Spirit of the Tinman

A True Story of Grace and Perseverance

Cherri Armstrong

Published by:
Gospel Armory Publishing
Bowling Green, Kentucky
www.GospelArmory.com

Printed in the United States of America

ISBN: 978-1-942036-98-2

Table of Contents

Introduction

The white cardboard box was nine by seven by five inches. On the label were his name and other personal information. I accepted it from the lady with some trepidation. I didn't know how I felt or how I was supposed to feel.

The mortuary employees kept referring to the box as "he" and "him," but I knew it wasn't him. I didn't know what the contents looked like but I knew, for sure, my husband wasn't in that small box. Still, I found myself talking to it occasionally. When I moved, I gently carried the box with me to my new home. It traveled in my car with me because it was my only physical representation of his presence.

A year later, on the first anniversary of his death, my daughter and I summoned the courage to finally open the box and view the contents. Inside the white cardboard box was a hard plastic box. We opened the lid to find a bag containing a fine, powdery substance, light gray in color. I was a bit surprised at the color and texture because I had never seen cremains before.

The crematorium had done its job well. His diseased, arthritis ravaged, scarred body was no more. Gone also, were the metal rods, screws, plates, balls and sockets that gave Jeff his self-proclaimed nickname of the Tinman.

There was no way to tell that this small pile of ashes had once been a human body made of flesh and bone, much less that it had been my husband. You couldn't see his smiling face when you looked at it. You couldn't feel his skin when you touched it. You couldn't hear his laugh when you held it to your ear. There was no possible way to reconstruct his physical representation from this little bag of dust.

In the same way, I cannot reconstruct his special spirit on the pages of this book. How do you condense the nature of a soul, the very essence of a life that God created, into mere words on a page? It is impossible. I know that I will fail miserably. Yet his life was so full of tragedy balanced with grace, power exhibited in weakness, and determination against all odds that the story deserves to be told. Not to honor the memory of my late husband (though I do), but in order to proclaim what God was able to accomplish through him.

I beg you, the reader, to look beyond the tragedy and pain you will see, especially in his early life. Instead, search for his indomitable spirit, fueled by God's grace and love. Try to catch a glimpse of one of God's most amazing creations, my husband, the Tinman.

Spirit of the Tinman

PART ONE

Once, A Little Boy
Named Jeff

"As He passed by, He saw a man blind from birth. And His disciples asked Him, 'Rabbi, who sinned, this man or his parents, that he would be born blind?' Jesus answered, 'It was neither that this man sinned, nor his parents; but it was so that the works of God might be displayed in him.'" John 9:1-3

CHAPTER 1

"Send Him Back"

Jeff was born on the evening of April 7, 1955. The temperature was a brisk 42 degrees that day with clear skies in Mill Creek, West Virginia. He was baby number six for Jack and Lelia Armstrong. It was a Thursday and there was no indication that there was anything special about this new baby boy.

In fact, his two sisters, Sharon and Delores, were disappointed that he was a boy. They already had three brothers, David, Ronnie and Tommy. They had wanted a sister to avoid being outnumbered. Sharon was 13 and Delores was nine at the time. They recall asking their parents to send him back.

This soon changed when Jeff turned out to be a cheerful, happy baby, always laughing and giggling. Delores recalls that he seemed to be the most loved of all the children but the others were never jealous of that because he was such a joy to them all.

In spite of that, or maybe because of that, he did have a mischievous streak. One favorite family story that got passed down was about Jack's alarm clock. It mysteriously went missing one day and Jack searched and searched, finally asking each of the children if they had seen it. Jeff eventually suggested "It *could* be under your bed, Daddy." It was. Jeff had hidden it there after breaking it.

Jack was a coal miner and, with eight mouths to feed, there wasn't a lot of extra money but the family enjoyed life's simple pleasures. They lived in town next to Bell's store, a small general store where Jeff could purchase candy. The playground was also down the street and the children often walked there to play with friends. Mill Creek was a small town where everyone knew everyone and parents could let their children play freely without worry.

They also enjoyed nature. In the spring, they would hunt for poke salad greens and in the fall, they would gather hickory nuts. Winter meant sleigh riding down Ward's hill and summer meant climbing trees, swinging from grape vines and playing in the creek. After looking for snakes, of course.

Another happy family memory was going up the mountain to get ice cold water, fresh and clean from a spring. Jeff loved playing and splashing in it.

The family "vacationed" at Aunt Velma's. She was Lelia's sister and lived on a large farm where the children loved exploring.

Jeff was also a rock hound. He loved finding interesting or unusual rocks. He was intelligent and inquisitive and this was one of his many pursuits. He carried that interest into his adult life, eventually leaving a small but varied collection for our grandson, who inherited the "rock gene" from him.

Being the youngest had its advantages. He loved doing things with his older siblings and they were good to him. David fashioned some kind of wooden box in a tree in the back yard and they called it Jeff's airplane. He spent a lot of time there and always remembered it fondly.

Jeff was three years old when Sharon got her driver's license. He loved riding around town with her. Those were the days before child safety seats. He would stand beside her on the seat while they drove and listened to the radio. His favorite song was "Wake up Little Susie" by the Everly Brothers. As he grew, his musical tastes became more sophisticated. His favorite band of all time was the Beatles.

Jack and Lelia also taught their children to be kind and generous. Jeff recalled one Christmas in particular when he was instructed to pick out one of his new toys to donate to the toy drive for less fortunate children. He gave away his new fire truck and learned the joy of giving to others. He was generous all of his life and the seeds were planted early.

He also saw their generosity in action. Lelia cared for her mother (Momaw) for many years, eventually moving her into a hospital bed in their living room. Jeff was Momaw's "tator bug."

In Jeff's memory, he was very athletic as a child. He could run faster, jump higher and spit farther than any of his friends. The truth of this may be partly verified by a story his best friend, Jack Currence, tells. According to Jack, Jeff could always outride him on a bicycle. This was in spite of the fact that Jeff had a small 20 inch and Jack was using a larger 26 inch (albeit an old girl's model). One day they were racing down the hill by the bank and Jeff passed Jack. Jack began peddling so hard to catch him that his bike broke in half. Jack had to pick up the two pieces of his bike and carry them home. He says he can still see Jeff laughing to this day. Jeff had a full, jolly laugh that was contagious.

Jeff always described his childhood as idyllic. These happy memories would have to sustain him in the hard years to follow.

CHAPTER 2

"I Can't Come Out to Play"

No child should have to suffer from chronic disease but sometimes they do. Jeff had routine childhood ailments but also there were early signs of something more. In hindsight it is easy to see what was happening but, at the time, the doctors were a little baffled and were simply treating symptoms.

As young as three, he was having severe nose bleeds. In December of 1964, at the age of nine, he was admitted to the hospital in Elkins with muscle pain and a "complete lack of energy." Frequent nose bleeds were also noted on his admission records. Based on the lab work, the doctor notes read "this child must be treated as an active rheumatic fever until proven otherwise." This was not exactly a diagnosis brimming with confidence.

Again in April of 1967, at the age of 12, Jeff was admitted to the hospital with painful, swollen joints. The physical examination indicated warm, swollen joints and a general paleness to his skin. The medical record from this visit is extremely interesting. It is obvious the doctors were still treating symptoms and guessing at a diagnosis. One note states "the child had an extremely stormy course" while in the hospital. The following is an excerpt from the medical record.

"His temperature each night would rise up to 104+. It started almost every evening at four o'clock and would spike at about 8 o'clock in the evening. This persisted for the first fourteen days in the hospital."

The admission notes suggested they should try to rule out rheumatoid arthritis but at the end of a 22 day stay and much lab work the final diagnosis was acute rheumatic fever. It wasn't until another hospital stay six months later that the diagnosis of rheumatoid arthritis was confirmed.

Rheumatoid Arthritis, or RA, is an autoimmune disorder wherein the immune system mistakenly attacks the body's tissues. It affects the lining of the joints but can also attack organs such as skin, lungs, heart, kidneys and various other soft tissues. It generally occurs bilaterally by affecting the same joint on both sides of the body at the same time. It creates pain, stiffness, fever and fatigue. It is not your grandpa's arthritis and there is no cure.

While the medical history is fascinating, this episode was devastating for a twelve year old just entering puberty. The nose bleeds and occasional bouts of listlessness had been a nuisance but they had been temporary. The occasional pain was no fun but, again it was temporary. This particular episode at the age of 12 was different. He knew it marked the end of his carefree childhood. This is how he remembered it.

He and his friends had been playing army after school one day. This apparently involved a lot of running up and down the foothills surrounding the town. That evening his ankles were so sore that he couldn't walk. He thought he was just sore from the strenuous playing but they never improved. Overnight he went from being an active little boy to being a sickly one who could no longer go out and play with his friends. By the end of that school year, he had been absent so many days that he was automatically forced to repeat sixth grade, in spite of his good grades. His friends and classmates moved on to the seventh grade which was housed in the high school building at that time. With this physical separation, the fragile bonds of childhood friendship were broken. He had now lost his health and his friends. At a time when most children are beginning to spread their wings, his had been clipped. How much more would this sweet little boy be required to give up?

CHAPTER 3

"There's a Problem at the Mine"

Jeff's father was a hardworking coal miner. During this time he was commuting over two hours away to a mining operation in Farmington, West Virginia. His habit was to drive to Farmington and "batch" with a buddy during the work week, then drive home for his off days.

Jeff and his father were always close but after Jeff became isolated at home Jack tried to fill the void left by the departure of his friends. Jack would take Jeff driving in his little gray VW Beetle. They would spend hours driving over the backroads in the surrounding mountains. Together, they explored nooks and crannies that most people overlooked. Those were some of Jeff's fondest memories and he spoke of them often. For the remainder of his life, as long as he was able, he enjoyed exploring country roads. Many times during our life together I heard him say "Let's see where this goes" as he turned off the highway onto an unfamiliar road.

Seeing what everyone else overlooked would be a trait that he carried throughout life. This was especially true about overlooked people. He felt overlooked for years and never wanted anyone else to feel that way.

I can only imagine what he and Jack talked about. Perhaps they didn't speak much at all. I do know that Jack's presence gave Jeff a sense of comfort and security as he fought his silent battle with his own body. These excursions were a welcome break from the monotony and loneliness he felt at home.

During this time there were regular visits to the hospital outpatient department for lab work, checkups and medication maintenance. He had been placed on steroids, pain medication and muscle relaxers and his condition had to be monitored. The medication only gave him minimal relief and made it difficult to stay awake in school. In addition, the steroids gave him the classic "moon face" often associated with steroids. Unfortunately, these were the only treatments available at the time.

By this time, Jeff's mobility had been reduced to the point of using, first a cane, and then forearm crutches. These crutches are the type with a cuff that straps around the forearm along with handgrips to grasp. He hated them because they always restricted his arm movements since they remained attached.

There is some indication in the medical record that these crutches also contributed to more bone damage. An x-ray report from 1972 mentions "old and adequately healed fractures" in his radius and ulna (the forearm bones). He never mentioned this to me and I suspect he never knew it. They were probably stress fractures from using the crutches. The pain would have been so close to the wrist that he assumed it was from the RA. This would not be the only time that his joint pain masked other problems.

When he was older he switched to the regular under-the-arm crutches. They would become his constant companions. In later years they became almost an extension of his arms. He would point with them, flip light switches with them and even pick items off the floor with the tips, using them like giant chop sticks.

Sometime in 1968, at the age of 13, Jeff was referred to the West Virginia University hospital in Morgantown. The physicians there suggested that some surgical procedures might benefit him. They recommended synovectomies of both wrists and both knees. This involved going into the joint and removing the synovium, a membrane in the joint that helps lubricate. In rheumatoid arthritis, the synovium overreacts as part of the faulty immune system and actually begins to destroy the cartilage in the joint.

Another, more drastic procedure that was performed was to surgically fuse both wrist joints. These surgeries left his wrists permanently frozen at a slight angle so that he could continue to use his hands for everyday tasks. This treatment of last resort seemed to help with the pain and, apparently, stopped the progression of the disease down into his hands. He retained the use of his fingers with only minimal restrictions up until his death 50 years later.

This long-term benefit came with a heavy price for a young boy, however. The procedure at this teaching hospital required that an extra-large, s-shaped incision be made on the top of each wrist so that pictures could be taken for further study. When he saw the incisions and realized he would bear those scars for life he broke down and sobbed. No one had explained what would happen. He couldn't understand why they would do that to a little boy. It was just one more blow to his damaged self-image. Those feelings persisted throughout his adult life. He very rarely wore anything but a long sleeved shirt in an effort to hide those long ago scars.

In this sea of physical pain and emotional struggle, the time spent with his father was the highlight of his life. That made what happened next even more tragic.

It was the morning of November 20, 1968. Jeff was in WVU hospital recovering from one of these surgeries. A few days earlier, his father had visited with him there. Jeff had noticed that Jack seemed distracted and he asked if anything was wrong. Jack brushed it off as just a problem at the mine. Jeff recalled that conversation as the events of this day unfolded. He would mention it every time he told the story of that day.

The first hint Jeff had that something was different about this day was that he noticed the nurses whispering quietly outside his room. They then came in and removed his TV with the excuse that it needed to be repaired. Jeff knew something wasn't right but couldn't get any answers.

At some point his doctor entered the room and told the nurses that "this boy has a right to know what's going on." They replaced the TV and the doctor explained that there had been a massive explosion at the mine where Jack worked. For the remainder of that day, this 13 year old boy watched the news in a hospital room with only the nursing staff for company. The family had rushed to the mine soon after they got the news early that morning so he was alone with his fears. He was desperate for news of his father's fate.

Jack had been right to be concerned for his safety. All of the miners had been complaining for weeks about hazardous conditions in the mine. Among other things, it was a very gassy mine and the ventilation fans which were supposed to send in fresh air and exhaust the methane were always breaking down. Many of the men, including

Jack, had been discussing the possibility of refusing to go back down until conditions improved. But they all had families to feed and needed the work. The men of the cateye shift had no way of knowing that their worst fears would be realized on their watch.

At 5:30 that morning Consolidation Coal Company's No. 9 Mine blew up from an accumulation of methane gas. There were 99 men underground at the time. Jack Armstrong was among them.

The families all gathered as near to the site as they were able. The company store and a small red brick church building soon became their refuge as they awaited word. Within 6 hours of the first explosion only 21 men had walked out or been rescued. 78 men were still trapped inside the burning mine.

The families would wait for 10 excruciating days before they knew that the fate of their loved ones was, quite literally, sealed. The mine had continued to spew flames, smoke and debris from every portal. As many as 20 additional explosions had been heard. The men in charge knew the only way to stop the underground inferno was to seal the mine and cut off the oxygen supply. They had promised the families they would not do that as long as there was a chance of life below. By day 10 they were out of options. Air samples pulled from bore holes indicated that the air inside the mine would not support life. There was no way to get rescuers inside. It was time to cap off the portals and vent shafts with massive amounts of concrete. Even then, some of the concrete caps were blown out with the continued explosions and had to be redone.

It would take a year for the mine to cool enough to send in recovery teams to search for the remains. Bodies were brought out over the next 10 years until the mine was sealed permanently, leaving the remains of Jack and 18 other men underground. Jack's little VW Beetle was left abandoned in the parking lot, along with vehicles of the other missing and dead men. The same little gray VW where Jeff had spent so many happy hours with his father was now the only physical evidence of Jack's death.

Jeff recounted this episode many times over the years but rarely discussed his feelings. I cannot imagine the pain and anguish he suffered over his loss. When you add to that the physical pain he was going through, it is a wonder he didn't lose his mind. But Jeff was always a strong willed individual and giving up was not his style. He would prove that over and over again throughout his lifetime.

CHAPTER 4

"I Want to Go Home"

Over the next few years there were more treatments, more medicines, more surgeries, and still, the terrible disease continued to ravage Jeff's body. He tried to continue his education but the high school building which housed his seventh grade classes was full of stairs. By the eighth grade he could no longer manage and the county began providing at home tutoring for a few hours a week. This education was sketchy at best and he finally was forced to drop out of the public education system. This was decades before the Americans with Disabilities Act was passed and there were few options. He took and passed the GED a few years later when his class graduated.

A few words need to be said here about Lelia. Her children describe her as always being joyful and full of laughter. That was also my impression of her when I met her years later. She was a wonderful mother-in-law and I loved her dearly.

During this time she was grieving over her husband, fighting the coal company (along with the other widows) for some form of compensation, dealing with Jeff's disabilities and trying to provide for Jeff and Tommy who were still living at home. In addition she had her own health issues. Somehow, with all of this going on, she managed to single-handedly raise a son that I was proud to call my husband. I don't know how she accomplished it but I will be forever grateful.

After Jack's death, Jeff and Tommy grew closer. They had always been close but Tommy, who was only 15 at the time, stepped in to fill the void which had once again appeared in Jeff's life. I don't know how they spent their time together but I know that Jeff always appreciated Tommy for being there for him. Sharon and Delores were both married and living a distance away. David and Ronnie were both in the armed forces and stationed elsewhere. They all visited when they could and helped out as much as they were able but Tommy was there every day helping out and being a companion for Jeff.

This family had been through so much together. They had faced their fair share of illness and grief but there was one more tragedy they would have to endure.

It was August of 1970 and Jeff was visiting with Sharon and her husband, Roger in Virginia. Sharon had always thought of Jeff as her baby because of the 13 year age difference. She frequently invited him to visit with her once she left home. On this particular occasion, Lelia was in the hospital and that may have been the reason behind this particular visit. Sharon and Jeff had ridden the bus from West Virginia so that he could stay awhile. Tommy did not make the trip because he had not been feeling well.

On that Sunday, they stayed home from church because of the toll the trip had taken on Jeff's body. Sharon and Roger did not have a phone at the time and the landlord sent a message by his son that they had a phone call at his place. Roger went to take the call and was gone for quite a while. Sharon and Jeff began to worry. When Roger returned he had his mother with him. He had taken the time to pick her up from church to help him break the news. Tommy had been killed in a pedestrian vs. car accident. Tommy was 17. Jeff was 15. Once again, his companion had been taken away.

They were all devastated once more. Details of the accident are hazy but Tommy had been struck by a car driven by his friends. He was airlifted to a trauma center. The family was told that his final words during the transport were "I want to go home."

Ronnie was stationed in Kentucky and was told by his captain that his brother was dead and he needed to go home. As a testimony to how sick Jeff had been, Ronnie just assumed that Jeff had died. He found out from the radio on the bus ride home that it was Tommy instead.

Jeff had now lost his friends, his father and his brother. The only thing he couldn't seem to lose was this awful disease that made his life miserable. It is not surprising that he admitted to me many years later that he became bitter for a while during his teens. But this attitude wouldn't last. Jeff was a fighter and he had a lot more fight left in him.

CHAPTER 5

"We've Had Enough"

Over the next three years, Jeff continued to have painful flare-ups. On two occasions he was admitted to the hospital when pain in his hip joints became unbearable and stiffness prevented him from walking, even with crutches. Both times he was placed in traction for a number of days. Physical therapy and hydrotherapy were also used to help ease the pain and stiffness.

At some point in time, he could no longer be carried up the stairs to his bedroom at home so Lelia had his bed moved to the dining room on the first floor. He was unable to sit down or rise up from a chair on his own. He needed help dressing because he couldn't reach his feet to put on socks, shoes, or even pants. Family members had to assist with these basic tasks. Momaw's bed was in the living room next door at the same time he was sleeping in the dining room. I'm sure he understood the sad irony of the fact that he was forced to live the life of the elderly, just like Momaw, though he was only a child.

Jeff spent so much time in physical therapy that they gave him an unpaid position, assisting with the bookkeeping for the department. His "can-do" attitude also made him a favorite of the therapists. He observed other patients that came in for treatment and could easily spot the ones who would improve and the ones who would not, simply based on their posture and attitude. He developed into a great judge of character.

While others gave up, he fought with everything he had, even with few options and a bleak future. In a letter dated June of 1973, one physician states, "I believe this patient is medically disabled for the rest of his life." Jeff was 18. This doctor obviously didn't know Jeff very well.

Sometime during 1974 Lelia and Jeff moved to Virginia. I don't know the specific conversation they had but when Jeff described it to me he said, "We've had enough." The once happy home had become a prison for Jeff and a reminder of too much tragedy for her.

The main advantage to the move was that it brought them closer to Sharon and Roger's family. Delores and her husband, Tom, also moved to the area later that year. Here, Lelia had more help and Jeff had more distractions. "Uncle Jeffy" soon became very popular with nieces and nephews. He joked and laughed with them and always had time to listen. He even made up a ridiculous password they were required to memorize and use whenever they wanted something from him. Much later, he made me memorize it, too. It was about 20 silly words all smashed together, guaranteed to make you laugh. Sorry, but it's still a secret.

The nieces and nephews loved spending the night with him. They made pizza or French toast together, listened to music and looked up at the stars at night. He allowed them to touch his scars and instructed them to not feel sorry for him. Being able to help with his special needs was an honor they fought over. He taught them to play chess and, best of all, he always listened. They loved him and looked up to him because of his great attitude. They were very proud when he began to preach later on. He inspired many of them to become faithful, active Christians as adults. As one nephew put it in a letter to Jeff, "I knew God was in our lives because He gave us you."

Delores' son, Brad, remembers Jeff helping him with a project for a history fair. They created a diorama of a Revolutionary war battle using scenery pieces from a train set. For the soldiers, they used Brad's little green army men. Jeff spent days hand painting each one, giving them either a red coat or a blue coat, along with white breeches and black boots. The affect was truly amazing. Jeff always paid great attention to detail.

The family time was a balm to his weary spirit. With them, he could be himself and if he was having a bad day he stayed in his room and they left him alone. They even made some trips together. One favorite memory is a trip they made to Rock City in Chattanooga. After enjoying part of the attraction, Jeff was tired and hurting pretty badly. Tom took him back to the car. They realized when Tom tried to help Jeff sit down on the seat that his legs were so stiff they had to just slide him in like a board. Even though Jeff was hurting they laughed and laughed.

This trip made an impression on the children as well. Brad remembers that Jeff and Tom made the five hour trip entertaining for them by telling silly stories. One of these involved trolls in the road. Every time the car hit a bump they claimed they were hitting a troll who had raised his head. The kids thought it was hilarious.

Jeff also enjoyed it when they came to help Lelia with yard work. He was always interested even though he couldn't help. One of his major regrets throughout our life together was not being able to work in the yard. He would have enjoyed it so much. With his attention to detail, we probably would have won the neighborhood beautification award.

Lelia had bought property from some of Roger's family and built a small, one-level house for her and Jeff. Jeff had his own room with a bathroom and the hallway was extra wide. The back door opened onto a patio with no steps. Everything was designed in anticipation of the day when he would be confined to the wheelchair that sat in the closet waiting for him. It would wait a very long time.

CHAPTER 6

"Take It or Leave It"

After moving to Virginia, a major life-altering event occurred, this time for the better. It would prove to be the most important decision of his life and also the thing that defined him. It would continue to mold him throughout his life.

The Armstrong family had always been good, church-going people. But they had never been truly convicted and committed with their whole heart. The move to Virginia brought them under the influence of Roger's family and other Christians who were committed to following the Bible at all costs. They began studying with two men, brothers in Christ, who tried to teach them the gospel straight from the Bible. They believed we should follow the Bible and only the Bible for all things spiritual and they could give book, chapter, and verse for everything they believed and taught.

Jeff had his own ideas that didn't always agree with their teaching. This is one time when his stubbornness almost became a detriment. After encountering Jeff's stubborn arguments again during one particular study, one of the brethren closed his Bible and said, "Well Jeff, that is what the Bible says. Take it or leave it." While that may sound harsh, it was exactly what Jeff needed to hear. After further personal study, he decided to take it.

On November 14, 1974, Jeff, Lelia and Delores were all baptized into Christ as described in Romans chapter six. Six years, almost to the day, that his world came crashing down with his father's death, he now felt whole again. He was accepted by other brothers and sisters in Christ and belonged to something bigger than himself and his illness. He now had hope of a better life in heaven one day. Most importantly, he now had a purpose in life and nothing was going to stop him.

He studied his Bible every spare moment. And there were a lot of those. He purchased Bible dictionaries, encyclopedias, Greek and Hebrew lexicons and commentaries. He spent most of his small disability check each month on more reference books. Roger, a carpenter, soon had to build floor to ceiling shelves in Jeff's bedroom to accommodate his growing collection. He spent countless hours on his bed with books spread out before him studying one topic after another.

After we married we moved his belongings to Alabama in my car. We stuffed books into every corner of the trunk and back seat. That blue Monte Carlo sat so low to the ground with its load that I wasn't sure we were going to make it home!

Studying wasn't all he did. He began taking his turn preaching at the small congregation where they worshipped. He stood behind the pulpit, propped up on two crutches, knees together to brace himself and the crowd never knew he was in pain. He went to prisons and nursing homes with other brethren in order to preach the gospel.

My favorite story is one that Jeff told about a trip up the mountain in an ice storm. He and another brother had agreed to go to a place called the Cove in order to show a set of evangelistic film strips to a small group of people. The Cove was way up in the hollows of the mountains and a narrow road was the only access. They were traveling in a VW Beetle and Jeff, being in the passenger seat, could look out the window and see a sheer drop off the side of the mountain. When the car began to slip on the ice, he began to calculate how he was going to get out of that moving car on his crutches before it went over the side! Fortunately, it didn't come to that.

Jeff never did anything without putting his whole heart into it and he had a big heart. Being a Christian was no exception. He was determined to serve above and beyond his physical ability.

CHAPTER 7

"Better, Stronger, Faster"

In the late 1970's, the doctors began discussing joint replacement surgery as a possible treatment for Jeff's worsening orthopedic condition. Revolutionary advances in technology over the previous decade made them hopeful that he would receive a good outcome. They decided to wait a few years to give his body time to achieve full growth before attempting this.

In November, 1979, when Jeff was 24 years old, they performed a total right knee replacement. This would be the first of four major surgeries over the next two years. Immediately, they knew they had a problem. Jeff was already under general anesthesia, unable to breathe on his own, when they discovered they could not intubate him. Intubation is necessary to provide an airway for the respirator which would keep him breathing during surgery. They were already using a manual resuscitator, or "bagging him," but they would have to act quickly or bring him out from under the anesthesia before he died. Another surgeon was quickly called in for consultation. He was able to use a fiberoptic scope to get around the problem and the surgery proceeded as scheduled.

The consulting surgeon notes indicate that the problem was caused by severe immobility of the cervical vertebrae due to arthritis in his neck. Additionally, the damage to his jaws prevented his mouth from opening more than two fingers high. Simply put, they could not position him in a way that enabled them to see the route for the tubing. Surgeons and anesthetists would battle RA before every surgery for the remainder of his life. (The jaw problem was a continual bane to him. He could never yawn to his satisfaction.)

In spite of the difficult intubation, the surgery was successful. The old damaged bones were gone and metal and plastic implements took their place. Almost immediately, he began physical therapy. The pain in his right knee was gone but he still had severe pain in the other joints.

After about three months of recovery they were ready to replace the left knee. Again, they had a very difficult intubation but the surgery was successful. He once again took therapy to strengthen the muscles around these new joints. Unfortunately, the tendons had shortened so much from years of disuse during his long illness that he was never able to achieve a full range of motion from his knees.

Reading the record for these procedures makes his body sound like a construction zone. Words like "sawing," "drilling," "reaming" and "cementing" are featured prominently. I cannot imagine what his body went through and yet, with each surgery another source of pain was removed.

In September of 1981 they performed a total left hip replacement and six months later a right hip replacement. Because of the difficulties they had encountered previously, they used a spinal block for anesthesia in both of these surgeries. This meant that Jeff was fully awake and talking as they cut into his flesh, sawed off the bones and pried them out of his body. He could recall the sound as his bones hit the disposal bin. He always told this story with amusement and perpetual amazement that he had actually experienced such extraordinary moments in his life.

Immediately after waking from this final procedure, he recalled feeling pain free in his legs. This is in spite of the fresh, 20 inch long incision in his hip that went all the way to the bone. This is one measure of how much pain he had been in previously. He had developed such a high tolerance for pain that he required very little post-operative medication.

With new joints and a lot of physical therapy, he learned to walk again. The hip replacements had left one leg shorter than the other and the damage to the tendons and muscles left him with an unusual gait and some limitations. He still used crutches, mostly for balance, and his movements were rather stiff. The stiffness combined with all the metal inside his body gave him the idea for the moniker, Tinman.

Even with his limitations, the doctors had made him "better, stronger, faster" (to borrow a phrase from a popular TV series of the time) than he had been since the age of 12.

All in all, he was in a better place than he had been in the last 15 years and in the best physical shape that he would ever be. He lost no time in making the most of it.

At the age of 27, he learned to drive and got his driver's license. That feeling of independence after being totally dependent on others gave him so much joy. He enjoyed driving for as long as he was able. Not only was it an escape from his past, but it gave him a feeling of control over his future that he had never had before. To be behind the wheel, deciding where he wanted to go was the exact antithesis of what he had experienced so far in his life. It was a perfect metaphor.

He had long ago been declared permanently disabled and was receiving a small disability check. Some men would have been totally satisfied with that. Not Jeff. He wanted to be productive. With that in mind, he enrolled in a nearby community college and began taking business courses.

Life was improving for Jeff. He had more freedom and friends and less pain but there was one problem still nagging at him. He was lonely. As God declared in the garden before He created Eve, "It is not good for man to be alone."

CHAPTER 8

A Prophetic Poem

Jeff always wanted to write down his own story. It proved too painful for him, both emotionally and physically. By the time that he retired on disability his body was in no shape to tackle such a project. In addition, it was very difficult for him to relive the tragedies, as he would have to do in order to tell the story.

He once told me that his title would have been "Once, a Little Boy named Jeff." It comes from a poem written by an aunt sometime during the worst of his troubles. He thought it was almost prophetic. I include it here to honor his wishes.

Once, a Little Boy Named Jeff

Every once in a while God makes a child different
    than all the others;
He lets him run and play awhile with his friends, sisters and brothers.
Then something happens to this child, no longer
    does he play and run;
I never mentioned how much it grieved me – how
    much I loved this little one.

For many years, I did not see him; but always in my
heart he stayed.

Through all his heartbreak, pain and sickness, I, with
so many others, prayed.

He journeyed through life's fiery furnace; like many
others have before.

But he never lost his faith in Jesus – each day he'd
fight; new strength restore.

As he grew older, and when I'd see him; I'd feel the
presence of the Lord.

The same most feel when they grow weary – a
blessed presence; the holy word.

For he walked through the storm of heartbreak; being tempered by the raging flame.

Knowing he had only Jesus – believing all in His
great name!

O, brave heart, you'll never falter; you'll win all your
battles, one by on.

For you're the kind the Lord depends on; - to you
one day, he'll say, "Well done!"

I know you're bored; so I'll stop writing; I would not
tire you all to death.

But I'm ever so glad I knew you – once a little boy
named Jeff!

By Aunt Mary Simmons

Jeff with Jack

Happy young Jeff in cowboy boots

Jeff with Ronnie and Tommy

Schoolboy Jeff before illness

Teenage Jeff after wrist fusions. Notice the scars on his hand.

Volunteering at physical therapy

Preaching on crutches

PART TWO

My Knight in Rusty, Dented Armor

"He who finds a wife finds a good thing and obtains favor from the Lord." Proverbs 18:22

CHAPTER 9

"Dear Sister Thomas"

The providence of God is a nebulous thing. Many times in our lives we may believe that God has had a hand in the outcome of a particular situation. On the other hand, providence is not provable like first century miracles because no natural laws are broken. Is it providence or is it coincidence?

Sometimes coincidences are so strong, so unusual, and so unbelievable that it is hard NOT to see God's hand. This was one of those times.

It all started when a visiting preacher was holding a gospel meeting in Jasper, Alabama where my family attended. I was living elsewhere at the time and was not present. At a social gathering in my uncle's home, the preacher was talking with my older sister, Oleta, and suggested she might be interested in a young man he had met a few weeks prior. It seems he recently held a meeting in Richlands, Virginia and had been invited to a meal at Lelia and Jeff's home. The view from Lelia's yard was spectacular because her house was halfway up a mountain. The preacher was showing pictures of the view which included Jeff in the foreground. When Oleta learned about his age and interests, she suggested that he sounded more like her sister, Cherri, than her. She passed along my address and promptly forgot to tell me about the conversation.

I was minding my own business, blissfully unaware of the entire incident, when I returned home from work one day and found a six page letter in my mailbox from a man I had never heard of. Well, it was a good letter so I wrote him back that evening. The following is a very short excerpt from this introductory letter.

"Dear Sister Thomas,

You, as of yet, do not know me. Your name and address were given to me by Brother Jimmy Thomas, who recently had a meeting for the Lord's people which assemble at Jasper, AL. Evidently through conversation with some of the good saints there concerning me, (apparently your sister among others) it was determined that it would be good for me to write you and introduce myself. So, with the opportunity afforded, I consider it a great privilege to correspond and get acquainted further with someone of "like precious faith." I will, of course, leave it to your discretion as to whether or not you wish to continue the correspondence."

This may sound stilted and formal to young people today but, to me, in 1982, it was a beautifully written letter, full of wonder and promise. He went on to describe his handicap, his preaching activities and other personal details. His honesty, intelligence, spirituality and good humor were evident on every page and I was intrigued by this letter out of the blue. Rest assured the formality did not last long.

Later, he would jokingly tell people that he sent out 500 copies and I was the only one to respond. I always pointed out that I was the only one to receive the original, hand-written copy.

We began writing frequently. This may seem an old fashioned form of courtship but it was perfect for us. In our letters we could delve into serious topics that allowed us to look deeply into each other's heart.

I had always been a bookworm and a bit of a loner. This was magnified by the fact that I grew up in the country with few close neighbors. As a result, I was socially awkward and had not dated very much. His physical limitations and my social awkwardness disappeared when we were writing. We got to know each other very well in a short time. No time was wasted on silly dating rituals.

We spoke on the phone occasionally but in those days, you paid by the minute for long distance calls. Neither of us was wealthy so we saved the calls for special occasions. We also exchanged pictures and cassette tapes. He sent me his taped sermons and I sent him tapes of music. We were using every communication medium at our disposal at that time.

This went on from August to November of 1982. By Thanksgiving we were anxious to meet face to face. I flew up for a visit and he met me at the airport where we shared our first kiss. It was his very first and he was always proud to tell people that I was the only woman he had ever kissed.

One funny story that he liked to tell on himself was that when he parked at the airport he locked his keys in the car because he was so anxious to see me. We discovered it when we went to the car after I landed. There, visible in my seat, was a single rose along with a card and we couldn't get to it. We laughed and he found a security guard to unlock the car. He told me later that he did the exact same thing when he returned me to the airport! The same guard helped him and mentioned that he looked familiar!

Despite the key incident, we were thrilled to finally see each other. The visit promised to be a good one.

CHAPTER 10

The Mountain of Love

I met his mother, Lelia, when I arrived that Wednesday afternoon. Jeff had been very discreet about our growing relationship. Lelia knew we were writing and that I was coming for a visit but not how serious we had become. I believe the rest of the family was totally in the dark.

Lelia warmly welcomed me even though I know she had to be a little concerned about Jeff getting his heart broken. His sisters and their families met me at Bible study that night and were probably flabbergasted but they hugged me in anyway.

Ronnie and David's families came in for Thanksgiving on Thursday so I officially met the whole family. I don't know what was said behind the scenes but everyone was gracious to me and I know Jeff was very proud.

After a big family meal that day, Jeff took me out to ride around in the car. We found ourselves (by design on his part) on top of the mountain where Lelia lived. Jeff pulled onto a grassy area and stopped the car. He told me to look in the glove box. Inside was a small square jeweler's box.

He had hinted on the phone prior to my visit that he might have a question for me and I had hinted that I might have an answer. I had no idea, however, that he had already purchased a ring. When we put it on my finger it fit perfectly, though he had no clue as to my ring size. We took it as a sign that we had made the right decision.

From that point on, Jeff always took pleasure in telling people that he proposed to me the day after he met me for the first time. This always required a telling of the story and people usually loved it.

In fact, we did not have our first "official" date until Friday after we became engaged on Thursday. He took me out to eat and to a movie. It was a magical time for us both. Thereafter Thanksgiving was always a special holiday for us. We always tried to spend it in Virginia with Lelia up until the time of her death.

Many people have commented that it sounded "just like a fairy tale." I suppose it did but he was no knight in shining armor and I was no princess, or even a damsel in distress. Instead, I usually referred to him as my knight in rusty, dented armor. He had faced down so many dragons before I met him that his armor was no longer shiny. It bore the marks of hard fought battles. But these battles had made him into the man he was and I loved him for it. In our youthful optimism we had no fear of the battles that might lie ahead and we began planning for our future together.

There was one more incident from that trip that became an inside joke for us. I had grown up in a large family that sat down at the table for meals together three times a day. Jeff and Lelia, on the other hand, had learned to eat around doctor and physical therapy appointments or just whenever they got hungry. We had eaten another large family meal on Sunday after morning worship services so when nothing was said about eating that evening I thought nothing of it. Monday morning he was preparing to take me back to the airport and, again, nothing was said about breakfast. I was too shy to ask so we began the long trip to the airport. By late morning I was beginning to get hungry and knew I had a long flight ahead. I got very quiet. He asked if anything was wrong. I asked if we were stopping for lunch before I boarded the plane. From then on, he knew he better keep me fed to keep me happy.

We hated to part but we were making plans to be together again over Christmas. Our memories and dreams would keep us happy until we met again. I stared at the unfamiliar ring on my finger the whole flight home. My seatmate, a perfect stranger, even commented on it. I had to tell her a short version of the story that never got old for us, even to this day.

The Christmas visit with my family in Alabama also went well. The only damper on the occasion was that my father had suffered a major stroke about the time that Jeff and I began writing. He was now in a nursing home mostly unresponsive. Jeff and I went to see him one day and I tried to tell Daddy about him but just received a blank stare. I don't know if he ever understood that I had found a good man. Jeff regretted the fact that he could not discuss the Bible with him. They would have really enjoyed each other but it was too late. Once again, Jeff missed out on a potential father figure in his life.

Daddy passed away just a few days after Jeff flew back to Virginia. I missed Jeff terribly during that time. Even with his physical limitations he would have given me strength as I grieved, just as he did years later at my mother's passing.

We continued our long distance relationship. The letters, cards and packages were flying through the mail. We later placed our letters in a scrapbook and the first few months are easy to follow as we took turns answering each other's letters. After that we were writing so frequently that they were crossing in the mail. This scrapbook is one of our most precious family treasures.

For Valentine's Day I received a shoebox full of construction paper hearts. They were different sizes and colors. Some had silly messages; some had poems written on them. Some were actually squares with the heart shape cut out in the middle. He said these were the negatives. I loved his sense of humor and the effort he put into it. Even wielding a pair of scissors would have been challenging for him.

Jeff continued his classes in Virginia and we began looking for a location where I could work and he could continue his education after our marriage. We were married in October of 1983 and settled in Tuscaloosa, Alabama where I found a job at a small private college and he could go to school. We would remain there for the rest of our lives together.

Our wedding was a simple but joyous affair. His mother, sister and nieces made the trip down for the ceremony. We were both excited to be beginning our life together. One of my favorite memories is when my sister-in-law hung a string of toy tin cans from his crutch in "just married" fashion.

We both knew when we married that his health would eventually deteriorate but we trusted that God would see us through it when the time came. That nearly occurred much sooner than we expected. While visiting at my mother's one day, his chair tipped over. She had ladder back chairs at her dining table and his chair caught on the rug as he attempted to rise from the table, sending him and the chair backwards. I had already left the table but heard the awful noise and turned around, my heart dropping to the floor. I thought that this might be it. When I reached him, he was still sitting perfectly in the chair, only on his back like a turtle. I leveraged the chair upwards and we discovered that he was totally unharmed. We laughed it off but it had scared us both and we realized, once again, just how fragile his body could be.

48

CHAPTER 11

School Days

I'm not sure exactly when it became clear in Jeff's mind that he was going to do more than take a few business classes. He had begun at the community college with the idea of perhaps getting a two year degree. Maybe it was the fact that he now had a wife that he wanted to support. For whatever reason, he became determined to get a four year degree in accounting. It would take everything he had.

He enrolled at the local junior college, Shelton State, as soon as the next term began. Because he had missed all of his high school courses due to his disability, he had to start out in remedial math and English. He soon caught up and was able to take courses for credit toward his degree.

He did well at Shelton State and was liked by his teachers and fellow students. He became active with Phi Theta Kappa, the junior college version of an honor society. After his first year there, he won a leadership award that came with a small monetary prize. We used it to buy him new shoes.

Jeff always wore special leather boots. They supported the top of his ankles, which were weak from the arthritis. They also had to be built up on one side because of the difference in the length of his legs as a result of the surgeries. They were not cheap and the cash award came in handy. My salary kept us fed and sheltered but we did not have money for extras. The best meal we ever had was one night when we opened our piggy bank where we threw loose change and discovered we had enough to order a pizza. We felt rich that night.

During this time also, Jeff began volunteering with the Arthritis Foundation. He led the local chapter and organized monthly meetings with speakers on various topics. As a result of his work we were able to take a trip to Nashville to attend a convention for the Foundation and we enjoyed the break from our routine. Annual trips to his mother's house for Thanksgiving were about all we could manage.

Although he stayed busy with school and volunteer work, he continued to study and grow as a Christian. We were meeting with a small, but dedicated group who had started a new congregation at Northwood just before we moved to Tuscaloosa. He took his turn preaching and teaching classes and it wasn't long before they asked him to preach regularly. He preached every Sunday morning and the other men took turns on Sunday nights. This continued until we found a full-time preacher to work with us. This also marked the first time he had accepted any payment for his preaching. In the past he had wanted to contribute his services to the work of the Gospel, just like the Apostle Paul, but now he reluctantly accepted support in order to contribute to the family finances.

One particular young man that he met in the congregation became a very close friend. Michael was several years younger than us but they had a lot in common. Michael suffered from Muscular Dystrophy and was already confined to a wheel chair when we met him. Like Jeff, he had a sharp mind trapped inside a dysfunctional body. They also shared a love of college football, particularly Alabama football. They spent many hours together talking and watching the games on television. Later on, Michael became the godfather to our daughter. It was hard for all of us when he finally succumbed to his disease. Still, Jeff managed to conduct the funeral service as Michael had requested. This was the only funeral service he ever performed.

Our church family was very important to us and we spent many happy hours with them outside of the worship services. There were several couples our age and we became lifelong friends. I believe this was the happiest Jeff had been since early childhood. Still, he felt a little inadequate compared to our friends. He was 28 years old and still had no degree, no job and no children. Most of our friends had all three. I'm not sure he ever truly got over those feelings, even though he accomplished so much. But that feeling of inadequacy never stopped him from trying.

He graduated from Shelton State and was ready to transfer to the University of Alabama to complete his degree. The university presented new challenges for him. Not only was the course work progressively harder but he was walking to class on crutches every day on a much larger campus. He could not wear a normal backpack so we made him a special book bag that he could carry while holding onto his crutches. He also spent many nights at the library studying. This was in spite of the pain and fatigue that still plagued him. The volunteer work stopped. It was all he could do to complete the necessary classes and I know there were times when others might have given up but he simply could not and would not.

Finally, in May of 1987, he graduated from the University of Alabama with a B.S. in Business Administration. He was the first of his family to earn a college degree, despite being the least likely to do so. The sick little boy who learned to walk again at the age of 26, now proudly walked across the stage at Coleman Coliseum on crutches to receive his diploma at the age of 32.

Sometimes degrees are conferred "cum laude" meaning "with distinction." Always one to see the humorous side of anything, Jeff told people he graduated "Oh, Lawd!"

Lelia traveled down for the occasion and I know she was very proud. There were a few days of celebration and then it was on to the next challenge.

CHAPTER 12

The Job Hunt

Jeff knew that few employers would want to hire a 32 year old rookie in the work force, much less one with a visible handicap. Still, he was disappointed when some of his more promising interviews didn't produce the results he hoped for.

As it turned out, it was all for the best. Most of those jobs would have required a long commute to Birmingham. A few weeks after graduation, he stumbled on a position with a nonprofit agency in Tuscaloosa. He had walked into their office on some other business but discovered they were about to have a vacancy. After talking with him for a good while they hired him on the spot.

He was so excited he stopped by my office to tell me all about it. After decades of hard work, both physical and mental, he had his first paying job. The physical therapy, difficult surgeries, hours of volunteer work and long nights spent studying finally culminated in the opportunity he had been waiting for. Now he wanted to prove himself.

He did well at the new job and enjoyed it very much. The position of Director over one of their volunteer programs gave him some valuable experience in his field and everyone in the small office loved him. The pay was not great but he was so thankful to be productive and bringing home a paycheck.

Sometime during this period, an occupational therapist introduced Jeff to some new tools. Specifically, he learned how to use a dressing stick and something we just called the "sock-putter-on-er." Obviously, this item could be used by him to put on his own socks by means of a flexible insert with straps. Once he stretched the socks over the insert, he would toss it on the floor and pull it over his foot by the straps.

The dressing stick was a multipurpose tool with a small circular hook on one end and a larger push-pull hook on the other. He used this to pull on his pants and shoes. We had a loop attached to the back of his shoes to fit the larger end of the tool. He could then use the smaller hook end to grab the zipper and zip them on.

All of this required more time than if I simply helped him as I had been doing every day since we married. The feeling of independence he got by finally being able to fully dress himself again was worth the extra time. Little by little he was feeling more "normal."

He was insistent that we purchase our first house. We were living in a mobile home that I owned before we married and I believe he wanted a fresh start in a home that was ours together. I wanted to wait and save a little more money but he continued to look. He was always more adventurous than me. I used to say that he gave me wings and I kept his feet on the ground. Maybe it was just his nature or maybe he was still making up for all the lost time. For whatever reason, once he made up his mind I gave in to the inevitable.

We found a small garden home and sold our mobile home. It was all one level with no steps and suited us perfectly. We enjoyed making it ours and spent many happy years there. At one time, Jeff had been contemplating a future spent in his mother's house, totally dependent on others. Now he owned his own home.

Not long after we moved in, Jeff had another career opportunity that was too good to ignore. Providence again? Maybe.

By this time I was working at the University of Alabama in the Financial Accounting office of the administration building. Across the hall from our office was the Contract and Grant Accounting office. They were expanding and had three entry level accounting positions to fill. Jeff interviewed and was offered one of them. The work at the nonprofit agency put him in a good position to be hired because of the grant experience he gained there. He hated to leave the small office but this was an increase in pay and great benefits that would come in handy later.

He was thrilled to be working at the University where he had graduated. The best part was that we were working across the hall from each other. We ate lunch together and saw each other frequently as we went through our day. We just laughed when some coworkers actually accused us of doting on each other. We felt that married couples should enjoy spending time together. Perhaps that sounds old fashioned but I still believe it is true. This arrangement continued for about five years until he transferred to another position at the University.

Jeff was a conscientious worker and would have been even without his limitations. He was taught to do his best at whatever task was before him. He felt the added pressure of proving that he could do anything a healthy person could do. He was naturally slower at moving than others and he could only use two fingers on a keyboard because of the arthritis. He gave everything he had to the job to make up for it. His job gave him a sense of worth and he loved working. It would gradually take a toll on his joints but, in the meantime, he was happy and productive.

The proximity of our jobs also made commuting easier since we only had one vehicle. On nice days we would sit in our car eating lunch. Parking was a problem on campus but with his handicap placard we could usually park close to the building. I sometimes teased him that I only married him for his handicap parking permit.

Jeff loved to tell the story of how one day we were sitting in the car and we saw a flower delivery being made to someone in the building. I made a wise crack about someone being lucky. He just ignored it. When we returned to our offices there were those flowers sitting on my desk. He just grinned and I felt about two inches tall. There was no special occasion. He just loved doing the unexpected. He was always good at keeping secrets.

CHAPTER 13

The Doodle

We had discussed having children but Jeff always had concerns arising from his health issues. There is no proof that RA is hereditary but susceptibility to certain triggers may be. In addition, he was concerned about the effect of all the chemicals that his body had been subjected to. He wanted children but was hesitant to saddle another generation with his problems. Added to this was the fear that his physical limitations might prevent him from being the father he wanted to be.

For once, I was the risk taker. I convinced him that we should trust in God and see what happened. He never regretted his decision. He came to know the joy and responsibility of fatherhood when our daughter was born in 1989. It was one more dream-that-he-had-never-dared-to-dream come true.

He was a wonderful father but you wouldn't know that by observing him in the delivery room the day Rachel was born. Jeff had a personality that naturally drew people to him and he was always talking to complete strangers. While I was trying to breathe through my labor pains, he was chatting with my nurse about this and that. I had to interrupt them to tell her I thought it was time to push!

It's not that he wasn't interested or excited. I think he just didn't know what to do to help so he did what he did best. I delighted in telling that particular story many times over the years.

Once they handed her to me we realized that she looked just like Jeff. From the minute he saw her she was Daddy's little girl. It was the first day of a very special bond they shared. He loved her with a fierceness only a father can know. He loved to make up silly nicknames. He called me "Cherri pie." He usually called her "the Doodle." I have no idea where he came up with that but it stuck. Another favorite of his was "Rachel Ree pocketful of glee." It was rather appropriate because Rachel was a happy child, much as he had been. That was just one more sign that she had inherited most of her genes from him!

His physical limitations hampered his baby sitting skills quite a bit but he did what he could. (Though he did manage to avoid changing all but three diapers during her infancy and did so then only because it was an emergency!) Simple things that many people take for granted took extraordinary exertion on his part. To get down on the floor to play with her required that he slide to the front of his seat, splay out his crutches on either side and lower himself to the floor by his arms. The reverse was required to get up off the floor. But he did this many times when she was small. I have no doubt that he enjoyed these simple pleasures more than most because he never expected to have them.

This is the way Rachel remembers it.

"Some of my earliest memories with my dad are playing with Barbies on the floor in my small, but light filled bedroom. At 3 or 4 years old, I had gone

into my bedroom to play with my Barbies expecting
to play alone. Dad came by and asked if he could play
with me. I, of course, said yes and was grinning from
ear to ear! I was old enough to know that, being a
boy especially, he probably did not want to play Barbies at all but was doing so to spend time with me. I
was sitting on the floor and waited to see where he
would go, thinking I would follow him and bring the
Barbies to him. While I didn't understand why, I
knew some things were harder for Dad to do and I
loved Dad and never wanted to make things hard for
him. I then watched as he sat on my bed and started
lowering himself onto the floor with his crutches. He
came to me! He never complained about being down
on the floor. I just remember us smiling and laughing
a lot. Despite his hard work and all the effort it took
to get down and back up, he seemed happy to do so. I
knew it was a selfless labor of love and that's how he
was."

"These were life lessons taught without saying a
word. When he did speak, there was usually meaning
beyond the obvious, wisdom behind the words.
What I remember hearing is a deep joy filled with
genuine laughter, but what I remember seeing was
someone who went to great lengths just to play with
me; great lengths just to do the ordinary. He lived in
the present and chose joy, despite the struggle. I always felt so fortunate that I was able to observe these
lessons every day from him. It made me sad that
those lessons came at the expense of discomfort and
pain."

"Another thing I noticed when I visited Dad at work was how he knew everyone's name, from his bosses all the way to the janitorial staff. It didn't matter what job or position you had, he knew you and would ask about your life and family. He would sometimes bring the maintenance staff doughnuts and you could see how much everyone respected Dad and appreciated being seen as a person. That was another of Dad's gifts. He could make everyone feel seen because he truly valued every single person he came across."

Another special time they shared was Saturday morning. Rachel would sit in Jeff's chair with him and they would laugh together as they watched cartoons.

When Rachel was nearly five, my mother became terminally ill. Jeff managed to care for Rachel on his own while I spent a few days and nights with my mother each week. I'm sure they helped each other during those times. He was a blessing and a support for me during Mother's illness and death. They arrived at her house just a few minutes after she passed away and it was such a comfort to me to see my little family just then.

When Rachel was old enough, he loved to take her places with him and show her off. He would take her to Alabama basketball games or to restaurants for a date. He was so proud of her!

When she was about eight, she was in a community children's choir. The night of her concert Jeff bought her a small bouquet of roses and surprised her with them afterwards.

Because they were so much alike, they understood each other in a way that I never did. They could talk about anything. I recall one evening especially. She was a young teen and we had a serious disagreement with her over something that I don't recall. We had gone to bed, leaving her in the dining room working on a jigsaw puzzle. Before we went to sleep Jeff got out of bed and put his clothes back on, which was a chore in itself. When I asked what he was doing he said, "I'm going to work a puzzle." I knew he meant more than the jigsaw. I never learned what they discussed late into the night but we had a peaceful household the next day.

Jeff loved to surprise her and make her laugh. Her favorite doll was named Lindsey and Jeff was constantly placing her in some unusual place, like on top of the curtains or the mantle. Then he would ask Rachel how she climbed up there. Rachel always giggled and so did he.

Then there was the time he created an elaborate treasure hunt for her sixth birthday. She had two friends over to spend the night and he left clues and a map for them to follow. At the end of the hunt he had buried a small wooden "treasure" box, complete with fake gemstones and real coins. The girls had a ball dividing up the loot!

The devotion went both ways. On a trip we made to Opryland one year when she was four years old, it was a sweet sight to see her holding his hand, "helping" him down some stairs. He normally took most of his meals at home sitting in the living room because it was easier on his body. As a toddler, she would run to him to take his plate asking, "Fru (through) Daddy?" She loved helping him.

We made many trips to Opryland when she was small. Jeff would find a show where he could sit while I took her on rides. Sometimes he even sat in the car with a newspaper while we had fun. He never wanted his limitations to hold us back. We all cried the day we heard they were closing that park.

We traveled to see family whenever possible and traveling with Jeff was always an adventure. He loved to make us laugh at silly things along the way. For instance, there was a small, one lane bridge on the way to my mother's. There was a sign that read "narrow bridge" but Jeff always read it as "nary a bridge." Or there was the section of mountain road on the way to Lelia's that had signs posted reading "congested area." He always pretended to go into a coughing fit when we approached that area. We always laughed because that silly joke never got old for us.

Of course, there was always the homemade fun. He would sometimes surprise us by driving past our driveway on the way home and taking us to the yogurt shop. Any time Rachel had a friend over he would find a way to take us for a "spin." This meant finding a large parking lot and driving the car around in tight circles while everyone laughed as the centrifugal force threw us to one side.

He always enjoyed life as much as possible. On one trip to West Virginia to visit his brother, we took a trip on Cass Scenic Railroad. We sat in an open car while the old steam locomotive chugged to the top of the mountain, then back down to the station. We were covered in soot by the time it was over but he had a ball being back in the mountains of West Virginia. I'm sure it brought back fond childhood memories.

On another occasion my brother, Kenneth, who was a pilot, took us up in a small plane. He allowed Jeff to take the controls for a short time and Jeff was thrilled.

He enjoyed the small things, too. He loved to stop at Cracker Barrel for breakfast when we were traveling. In fact, he enjoyed it so much that he would sometimes drive to the restaurant in Tuscaloosa after a Sunday or Wednesday night Bible study just so we could sip hot chocolate and snack on biscuits.

One of his favorite things though, was Christmas time. He enjoyed seeing us all open presents on Christmas morning. He usually had wonderful ideas for gifts but hated shopping so Rachel and I assisted with the shopping and wrapping. Of course there was the year that he gave me a tool box for Christmas. I had requested it so I was happy but he loved telling his coworkers about it just to see their reaction.

And then there was the year that "Daddy ruined Christmas." Rachel was about nine and Christmas happened to fall on Monday that year. He thought it was a shame that Rachel couldn't enjoy her new things over the weekend and suggested that we open presents early on Friday. Rachel, being a child, thought it was a great idea. I knew it wasn't but I got outvoted.

Everything was great until Sunday morning when Rachel saw her friends at church and realized that they were full of anticipation for Christmas morning and hers was already over. She was so upset that we decided we had to have some small gifts to open the next morning. I took Rachel to a store and gave her a few dollars to shop for me while I found some small items for her and Jeff. We enjoyed a downsized Christmas morning. We laughed about it later but never again did we open presents early.

While he loved to laugh, he could be deadly serious if circumstances warranted it. He never spanked Rachel but he didn't have to. One look from him and she would realize he meant business.

Spiritual matters were never far from his mind. They even crept into his dreams. One morning he asked me what were the three most important words ever spoken. I had no idea where this conversation was headed but I took a guess. He then explained that he had a dream the previous night where he met the smartest man in the world and asked him the same question. The smartest man in the world didn't know the answer either. Jeff then gave him a profound answer. He told him the three most important words ever spoken were "He is risen." As you can see, he had his priorities in order.

Rachel continued to look up to her father and helped whenever she was needed. I recall one Sunday morning when Jeff fell while dressing for worship service. She was a teenager but between the two of us we still could not lift him safely. The three of us put our heads together and came up with a plan. Jeff scooted into a seated position on the floor in front of a blanket chest. Using his crutches, he pushed himself a few inches off the floor. Rachel and I shoved a storage box underneath him. We repeated this process over and over using books, pillows and anything we could find until he was high enough to sit on the chest. From there, he could get to his feet.

Life with Jeff was always interesting.

CHAPTER 14

Wear and Tear

Jeff had been so grateful for the joint replacements that allowed him to live a semi-normal life but they were not magic. They could not undo all the damage done to his body and they did not send the RA into remission. This terrible disease continued to attack other parts of his body in spite of the anti-inflammatory drugs he took every day.

In the spring of 1996, Jeff was experiencing sharp pain between his shoulder blades and numbness in his right hand fingers. Being his usual tough-it-out self, he put up with this for a few weeks before seeing an orthopedic surgeon. The diagnosis was a pinched nerve in his neck resulting from arthritic damage to his cervical vertebrae. The only solution was surgery to fuse three of his vertebrae together with a metal plate. The surgery was difficult but successful. After several weeks in a neck brace, which further limited his movements, he was ready to get back to work. He would fight a continuing battle with his neck for the rest of his life.

None of this diminished his eagerness to work hard at his job and serve the Lord with all his strength. He served as a deacon in our congregation during these years, taking on many tasks in addition to teaching Bible classes frequently. One of his projects was to create a series of pamphlets designed to be used in evangelism.

He was determined to take advantage of every opportunity while he still could. The artificial joints were nearing the end of their expected life of 15 to 20 years. He knew time was running out.

Friends and co-workers never knew the war he fought with himself every morning just to get out of bed. He could barely function until after a hot shower loosened up some of the stiffness each day. And still he worked.

There were times when I begged him to slow down and go on disability but he refused. He wanted so badly to work the full 25 years until retirement from the University that he simply would not give up.

There were other times when I tried to persuade him to use a wheel chair part-time in order to save the wear and tear on his joints. Again, he refused, fearing that if he ever gave in to using a wheel chair he would never get out of it.

Many of his doctors over the years offered to certify his total disability but he declined them all. Meanwhile, the clock was ticking on those old artificial joints.

Instead of slowing down, he found yet another way to serve our congregation. He was appointed to serve as an elder and joyfully accepted the responsibility. He felt he had a small window of usefulness left and he wanted to make the most of every minute.

Aside from his family, I believe becoming an elder in the Lord's body was, to him, his crowning achievement. It was not because of any honor accruing to him from the office but because he felt it was the ultimate way to serve his Lord. He took his duties very seriously and worried and prayed over his sheep. He sometimes found it hard to express the depth of his feelings and I doubt any of the congregation knew just how much he cared for them. They certainly didn't know how much it took out of him physically.

By this time it had become so difficult to walk that he went to work and sat at his desk all day without getting up. He avoided drinking anything while there so that he would not have to walk to the restroom down the hall. Once home, he fell into his chair until he could summon the strength to walk to the bedroom. And still he worked and served.

In the past, we had shared meals with friends in each other's homes or in restaurants and traveled to see family as much as possible. Now all he could manage was work and church responsibilities. He had no energy left for anything else.

We still traveled to Virginia to see his family when we could. One trip he made with Rachel. For some reason I couldn't travel at the time and it was just the two of them. This is Rachel's account of the trip.

> "One year I got to take a special trip all by myself with my dad. I was thrilled to have the opportunity to spend extra time with him, just the two of us. One of the many things we had in common was our love of food. We joked to Mom that we were going to eat our way through every state on the way to Grandma's. We both had a terrible weak spot for junk food; chips, candy bars, and our favorite – pepperoni. Yes, just plain pepperoni slices. While we didn't really stuff our faces with only junk food, we did make the

occasional stop at a gas station to get a treat. Dad's favorite was Payday candy bars, the salty-sweet caramel nugget bars covered in peanuts. He usually only ate them on trips to Grandma's. He also allowed me to pick out my own special treat – usually a Ya-hoo and a crunch bar, or beef jerky. I know these weren't exactly a nutritious snack but Dad liked to occasionally splurge on something we would typical-ly never do."

"I loved taking care of Dad and this trip was a great opportunity to do that. Just getting into the car was a whole process for him because of the limitations of his neck, back, and legs. Each time we stopped for gas, I would get out of the car and go around to the other side where his crutches would be stacked just so on top of the back seat. The tops always faced the door behind the driver's seat in case he needed to get them out by himself in an emergency. Dad always had to think through every detail of what we might see as typical or simple everyday tasks. While I did that, Dad would use the lever on the bottom left side of his seat to push his seat all the way back. Once he had room to exit the car, I would hand him his crutches. The screws always had to face the back so they could not get caught on his pants pockets and cause a fall. He would take them and, as gracefully and gently as he could, slide out, bracing himself on his crutches."

"While we laughed so hard and had so much fun, I couldn't help but notice him struggling. Watching him get in and out of the car just broke my heart but I could only do so much to help him. I could see him grimace in pain and try to cover it up. It became much worse the day we went to visit my aunt's house."

"Aunt Delores' home was beautifully nestled into the mountains and I always loved visiting. Beyond their garage, on the left side under an awning was the entry to their house. Three large and steep concrete steps lead to the door. Every time Dad climbed or descended stairs, I held my breath, knowing that a fall could be really dangerous for him. I watched him study these steps. I could tell he was a little nervous about how to reach the top. He planted his crutches on the ground and swung upward trying to reach the first step. He didn't quite reach it and swung backward, nearly falling, but stabilizing himself with his crutches. He tried again and pushed off, landing hard atop the step. I heard him make a noise and watched his face as he tried to mask the pain and worry. He immediately knew something was wrong. Dad always tried to cover up his worries, but I always knew. He happily visited that day but was moving a lot more slowly and differently than normal. There was a quiet worry behind his smile and laugh. After we left that day, I asked him and he said he felt a pop and his leg was hurting badly. Watching him get in and out of the car became even more painful to watch for the remainder of the trip."

When Jeff and Rachel returned home, I knew he was hurt. I could tell he was worried about it, though not enough to see a doctor. He thought he could rest it and it would improve. When it didn't, he simply stopped weight bearing on that side by leaning more heavily on his crutches. This would prove to be a momentous decision with far reaching consequences later on.

We made another trip in 2005 when Lelia passed away. Jeff was left in charge of her estate. He took care of arrangements and business as he had done a few years earlier when his brother, David, passed away from cancer. The family knew they could count on him for leadership during hard times.

It was a sad and busy time but, as usual, he kept his sense of humor. Going through Lelia's belongings after the funeral, we found a prescription bottle with some of the same pain tablets he took. He brought them with us when we left since he already had a prescription. We were also traveling with a good bit of cash. We joked all the way home that he better not get pulled over for any reason because they would arrest us for drug trafficking!

He was still the same Jeff but it was getting harder and harder to fight the daily battles. The losses and the pain were mounting and his mobility was deteriorating.

CHAPTER 15

Facing Reality

The year 2007 would prove to be a busy one for us. Rachel was graduating from high school and we were looking for a smaller house. We had lived in an older house for 14 years and it was great for entertaining but those days were almost over. We needed something smaller and newer that would be easier for me to maintain.

We had found another garden home and were in the process of selling our old house when Jeff reached the decision that he could no longer carry out his duties at work or at church. I don't know what the deciding factor was for him but I was glad. He had worked for 20 years at the University and could retire on disability. He resigned from his duties as an elder. We moved, Rachel graduated and he retired all within a few weeks.

He hobbled to Rachel's graduation exercises but had to miss the remainder of her senior activities. Graduation itself was an ordeal for him. During the ceremony, the parents were expected to walk down to the front while a personal message was read from our child. Rachel had been living this crazy life with us for 17 years and never expected him to make the walk. She was surprised and elated when he made it. She knew how much effort it had taken.

In fact, many years earlier, Jeff had apologized to her for not being like other dads when he couldn't sit on the bleachers and watch her soccer games. I found out much later that they had this conversation various times throughout the years. Rachel always assured him that, in her eyes, he did more for her than all the other dads. He spent time with her and they talked about everything. She learned so much from him.

He had received his disability from the University but was required by the insurance company to file for his social security disability as well. When he received it, they would decrease the amount he was receiving from the University insurance. In order to expedite that, the insurance company paid for a consulting firm to assist with filing the social security disability claim. Jeff filled out pages and pages of questions about his daily life, mobility, limitations, etc.

A strange thing happened when he filled out that questionnaire. He filled out a rough draft first and asked me to read over it. I noticed that he was putting the most positive light on his situation as he had always done. Instead of "I can't shave every day" he had written "I don't shave every day" and so forth for every question about his activities. The word "can't" had been expunged from his vocabulary for a very long time by sheer determination. I pointed out that, for the purpose of this document, we had to be brutally honest. We could no longer afford to minimize what was really happening. He agreed and reworded his answers to reflect reality but I think it cost him emotionally. It was so hard for him to admit defeat.

He asked nothing more for his retirement than that we be there with him on his last day of work. Rachel and I went to help him gather his personal belongings and say goodbye. He cried. He understood, better than we did, that the future was a lot dimmer than it had been before. Being useful and productive had given him self-worth and he was going to have to adjust to being labeled as "disabled" all over again.

He spent the next several months completing paperwork for his retirement and disability. He also supervised the building of a deck in our back yard where he would be able to sit and enjoy the landscaping he had hired done. The deck was level with the back door so he could easily access it. It had a ramp down to the back yard.

In fact, it was supposed to be just a ramp. I left for work one morning as he was planning a ramp from the back door with our friend who was going to do the work. When I came home that afternoon, he had expanded the project to include a large deck. I always told people that I didn't have a deck. I just had a ramp with a BIG landing!

One way and another, he managed to stay busy that summer and autumn. He didn't leave the house much but he was adjusting and learning to be content again.

By this time Rachel was getting serious with a fine young Christian man she met at church. Andrew asked Jeff for Rachel's hand and they became engaged at Christmas. Now Jeff had a new project. We had a wedding to plan.

CHAPTER 16

Father of the Bride

The wedding date was set for August of 2008. Jeff, of course, didn't do the actual planning. His role was more advisory and counseling. He also helped search for bargains on the internet. He became quite good at researching and shopping online because he spent a lot of time on the computer after retirement. Being confined to a chair most of the day, it became easy to lose himself in the computer.

We loved Andrew and were happy with their decision but they were both young. Jeff took extra care in providing them with spiritual resources and advice on marriage. I'm sure he had mixed emotions about being the father of the bride but he was happy.

One thing that concerned him was how his physical limitations would impact some of the traditional wedding activities. For instance, he knew he could never wear a traditional tuxedo with his crutches. He gave the problem a great deal of thought and came up with a creative, typically Jeff, solution.

The Armstrong family originated from the Armstrong clan in Scotland. They were among the border clans which served as a buffer between Scotland and England. As a result, they were heavily involved in the battles between these two nations during the 13th and 14th centuries. The clan motto was, appropriately enough, "Never

Vanquished." Perhaps that is where Jeff's fighting spirit also originated.

As a nod to his Scottish heritage, he ordered a special garment called a fly plaid. This is a traditional Scottish piece of tartan about 54 inches square. One corner is laid over the left shoulder and attached with a plaid broach while the remainder falls down the back. He ordered a fly plaid in the Armstrong tartan and a broach with the Armstrong crest. He wore this over the tuxedo vest and his own white shirt and black pants. The overall look was formal and distinguished yet with a little Jeff flair. We loved it.

The next hurdle was actually walking her down the aisle. She chose to have the wedding outside in the yard of a beautiful old manor house. They would walk up a brick paved sidewalk to the steps of the front porch where he would hand her over to Andrew. The uneven brick path went slightly uphill to the steps. This could have been an accident waiting to happen.

One of my favorite wedding pictures is of the two of them proceeding up the aisle. Rachel is looking toward Andrew with joy and excitement. Jeff is walking with a very determined look on his face. Anyone who didn't know might think he was unhappy. Actually, it was just the opposite. He was trying not to ruin the day by tripping and falling! Rachel, of course, was not concerned about her day being ruined, only Jeff's safety.

The problem of the receiving line was solved by bringing a stool for him to sit on or lean against as he had need. He greeted every single guest and made it through the reception with a smile, though I know he was hurting badly by the end of the night.

He had done his part admirably and we loved him all the more for the extra effort he made. He had even helped me prepare the guest favors. He and I sat at the kitchen table one day working on them. He was placing the candies in the small circles of tulle while I tied them with tiny ribbons. He seemed fascinated by what I was doing and finally asked me how I did it. I realized that his fingers had not been able to do delicate tasks in over 50 years and I loved him for making whatever contributions he could towards the success of that special day.

That October was our own 25th wedding anniversary. Jeff tended to show his devotion in occasional grand gestures rather than in small, every day moments. For our 10th anniversary he gave me a framed poem that he had written. It still hangs in my home. For our 15th we made a trip to Natchez to stay in a historic mansion. While there he made a supreme effort to climb into a horse drawn carriage with me for a tour of the historical district. For our 25th he was still feeling drained from the exertion of Rachel's wedding so we celebrated quietly at home. That became our routine from that point forward.

Jeff and I had become empty nesters. I was still working and he was home full time. He kept busy with hobbies, mostly at the computer. He had a coin collection when he was younger and never lost interest in numismatics. He began another collection and spent hours on the internet chasing down the best bargains. He also conducted Bible studies in our home whenever possible.

One of these was a study he had with Rachel. She was in school and a young bride but still found time to visit with Jeff every week. Since I was at work during the day, I missed out on these visits and the class on Zechariah they did together. Rachel cherishes that time she had with her father.

He held another weekly study with one of our elders and a young preacher who came to work with us at Northwood. It was on the book of Ecclesiastes with study material he put together himself. The men who participated talked about it for many years.

He was keeping busy but was lonesome with me at work all day. He was about to find a solution for that.

CHAPTER 17

Lilli

Jeff always loved dogs. Lelia had a black cocker spaniel named Missy when he was young. Missy brought him a lot of comfort when he was so sick and confined at home. We had two different silver toy poodles during our years together but they were both gone and I thought we were through with dogs. After all, I was at work all day and Jeff could barely get out of his lift chair for his own needs. He certainly couldn't house train a new dog. Then he spotted Lilli.

He "accidently" found her while looking on the internet for something else. At least that was his story and he was sticking to it. She was another silver toy poodle and was up for adoption. She was four years old and house trained. Her family could no longer keep her and she was being placed by a rescue agency.

When he first mentioned it to me, I was totally against the idea. I thought I had enough to do between working and taking care of his needs. He reminded me how much company she would be for him while I was gone and I began to cave. I could never deny him anything that might bring him some measure of comfort. We decided to apply.

Jeff contacted the agency and filled out the paperwork. I was amazed at how much effort they made to find the right placement for

Lilli. After all, she was a dog, not a royal heir, but finally we were cho-
sen and Jeff was excited to get her.

We would have to drive about two hours across the state to meet
her and we decided to make an evening of it. Jeff had difficulty getting
in the car but once in, he was comfortable driving. We rarely went
anywhere by this time and thought we would take the opportunity to
eat at a restaurant before meeting the rescue people.

We ate at a Cracker Barrel near the rendezvous point. After the
meal, Jeff found it impossible to get out of his chair, even with my
help. His crutches kept slipping on the floor and he could not get
enough leverage to help me hoist him up. Our server came to the rescue and lifted from behind while I pulled from the front. We managed to get him to a standing position but it would be the last time he
ever ate inside a restaurant.

This trip was also one of the last times he ever drove. We had
tried many different vehicles over the years, trying to find one that
was easier for him to use. Several years prior to this he had found one
that he loved. It was a small SUV that was high enough for him to get
on and off the seat without too much strain. It also had leather seats
that made it easier for him to slide in. He even ordered a personalized
license plate with the name "T1NMAN" where the "1" substituted for
the "I." Appropriately, it was a white Ford Escape. It certainly represented an escape for him.

In spite of the difficulty at the restaurant, the meeting with Lilli's
handler went very well. Lilli was a well behaved dog who loved people
and she came to us without a second thought. She loved to ride and
was excited the entire trip home. When we arrived at our house, she
trotted up the steps and waited for us to open the door. Once inside,

she went straight to the water bowl we had left out. She acted like she had lived with us all of her life.

She slept through the night on our bed and soon fell into our routine. She wasn't sure about Jeff's motorized lift chair at first. She was a little skittish about sitting with Jeff because every time he moved she thought the chair was going to move and she would hop down. She eventually adjusted to that and became his constant companion.

We got Lilli in mid-April of 2011. A week later, on April 27th, a devastating tornado cut a mile wide path through Tuscaloosa, destroying thousands of homes and businesses and killing nearly 50 people.

Living in Northport, we were spared and never even lost our electricity. We watched it unfold on the news as we worried about how our friends were faring. We soon found out that some had lost their homes and one of our young friends from church, a college student named Marcus, was missing.

Efforts were made by everyone at church to find him while Jeff and I sat home and prayed. His body was finally found in the rubble five days later and we were grief stricken. We mourned with his family and friends. At the same time, we were so thankful that we had not been in the path of the storm. The reality of our situation was such that I could never have moved Jeff into a sheltering place in time.

We had been protected from the tornado but we were about to face our own, very personal storm.

Engagement weekend – We're in this together

University graduation with Lelia

New father

Playing with Rachel

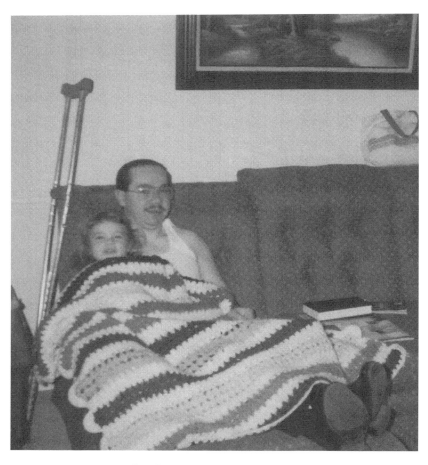

Jeff and Rachel watching cartoons

Father of the bride

At home while still ambulatory

PART THREE

Power Perfected
in Weakness

"For to me, to live is Christ and to die is gain. But if I am to live on in the flesh, this will mean fruitful labor for me: and I do not know which to choose." Philippians 1:21-22

CHAPTER 18

Without a Leg to Stand On

In Second Corinthians chapter 12 the Apostle Paul relates how he prayed for the removal of a "thorn in the flesh" three times. The Lord answered him, "My grace is sufficient for you, for power is perfected in weakness." I don't know how many times Jeff prayed over his personal thorn in the flesh but I believe the answer was the same. God's power was shown in Jeff's life over and over again, but never more plainly than in his final years. It seemed that the weaker Jeff's body became, the more God's power was revealed through Jeff's spirit.

On Monday evening, June 6, 2011, just six weeks after the tornado, Jeff fell in our bathroom while getting ready for bed. He knew his remaining "good" leg was injured but we didn't know to what extent. I called two young men from church to help me get him into bed since I could not lift him. Jeff instructed me to strap his legs together using some ace bandages to support them for the move. Once he was in bed, we assessed the situation. He thought that he had pulled some ligaments or other soft tissue and it would heal with a little time. As usual, he had become so accustomed to pain that he didn't realize the seriousness of the injury.

Rachel and I had planned a girl's trip for the end of that week and he was determined that we should go anyway. I certainly wasn't going to leave him in that condition and told him so. With that in mind, he attempted to get out of bed on Wednesday after resting all day on Tuesday. He leveraged his body out of bed onto his crutches but when he attempted to put weight on his legs they gave way and he fell back on the bed.

For once, sheer determination wasn't enough. He literally did not have a leg to stand on. The newly injured right leg wasn't holding him and he had stopped weight bearing on his left leg all those years ago when he injured it on the trip to Virginia.

He sat on the bed and looked at me. I had never seen him look so defeated. In a rare moment of weakness he proclaimed that he wished he was dead. I was a little shocked to hear him say those words because he nearly always had a positive attitude. I could see he needed me to carry the emotional load a little while. I said, "Well, you're not so we'll have to figure this out together."

I made him as comfortable as possible in bed and we talked. He finally agreed that there was no other option than to go to the emergency room, but only on his terms. Since it wasn't a life-threatening situation he wanted to wait until the next day to call the ambulance. He wanted time to prepare his mind for what might happen next. Also, he wanted time for me to clean him up a little before going to the hospital. The least I could do was help him salvage a little dignity so I agreed.

Rachel came down on Thursday and traveled with me to the hospital while Jeff went by ambulance. They took x-rays of both legs and then the three of us sat in an ER cubicle. We discussed the possibilities while we waited on the doctor. The actual diagnosis, when it came, was something we never dreamed of in all our speculation.

The young doctor entered the room and I could tell he was uncomfortable with what he had to tell us. His first words were, "We have a problem." He hesitantly told us that Jeff had two broken legs. Both femurs were fractured. Our reaction was probably not what he was expecting. We looked at each other in surprise and admitted that we had not thought of that possibility. There was no complaining or hand-wringing or any other sign of self-pity on Jeff's part. He had been through so much that this just became the next hurdle to jump. His mind was already envisioning the long road to recovery. I'm sure the doctor was surprised but relieved when we calmly asked what should be done.

The doctor went on to explain that the right femur was a fresh break from the fall. The left femur had been broken many years before. We suddenly knew exactly what had happened that day at Delores' house. On the x-ray we could see a large knot of bone where it had tried to heal over and over again. It could not fuse because it had not been properly re-aligned so it just kept slipping apart. We immediately thought back to that long-ago trip to Virginia when he had injured his leg. We realized that he had been walking around on that broken bone for years. Not only that, but he had tried to stand up the previous morning on two broken legs. He was unable to do so, but the fact that he had tried was astonishing. Once again, he had underestimated the extent of the injury because of his high tolerance for pain.

Because of his complex orthopedic history it was decided that he should go to a specialist in Birmingham. I sometimes wonder if that young ER doctor remembers the case of the two broken femurs. We never forgot his name. It was Dr. Pepper. I can't make this stuff up.

Jeff was taken by ambulance to UAB where he met with a surgeon who specialized in joint revisions. That is the procedure where an existing artificial joint is removed and replaced by a new one. In Jeff's case the surgeries would be more complicated because he had already lost so much bone in the previous replacements and the bone tissue that remained was damaged. There was no place to attach the new joint. The only solution was to remove the old joints and broken femurs and attach a new hip joint along with a metal rod, essentially an artificial femur, to the top of his artificial knee joints.

Jeff agreed to have the surgeries but, once again, on his terms. He wanted to wait about a month before beginning so that he could get his affairs in order and prepare mentally for the long, hard road ahead of him. The surgeon agreed and Jeff was taken home by ambulance.

We had always been in this endeavor together but this new circumstance forced our reluctant physical separation. Now I had to move into the guest room to make space for the hospital bed, patient lift, motorized wheel chair and other equipment he would need for an extended period of rehabilitation.

He had purchased the power wheel chair after he retired on disability. Aside from a few test runs it sat unused in our house. Now he used it every day. Using the patient lift, I could get him out of bed and into the power wheel chair where he spent the day while I was at work.

While waiting for the first surgery, he prepared both his Will and his Advance Directive, which provided final health care instructions. He did not wish to be resuscitated if something went wrong during the long procedure. He was ready to go to his eternal home if that was the outcome. At the same time, he planned for a good outcome by researching possible facilities for his postoperative rehab. Once he was satisfied with his preparations, it was just a matter of waiting for the scheduled surgery.

CHAPTER 19

More Surgery

Oddly enough, though Jeff was now in a wheel chair, he was more like himself than he had been since he retired. For the last few years he had been trying to find ways to stay busy but without much purpose. He now had a new goal and a plan to achieve it. He always had laser focus when he wanted to accomplish something and this time was no different.

His new goal was to learn to walk for the third time in his life. He, of all people, knew how much work was involved but I believe he looked forward to the challenge. It was another chance to prove himself. He warned me that it might take years. I told him I was there for him regardless of how long it took. When we married I vowed that I would never leave that little boy behind again and I meant it.

We went back to UAB in late July for the first of what was supposed to be two surgeries. They had decided to do the right hip revision and rod insertion first because that leg was in better condition since he had been using it up until the fall in June. After that leg healed and became stronger they would do the other side.

The surgery went well after initial problems with the anesthesia. Not only did they have the same old problems with the intubation but they had difficulty finding a vein for the IV. He had always been a difficult "stick" but it grew worse after all the procedures his body had endured. In addition, his elbows did not have full range of motion and his arms did not straighten all the way. They finally found a vein in his foot and proceeded with the successful surgery.

The surgeon saved the original prosthesis and gave it to us afterwards. He commented that it should be in a museum. That piece of steel had lasted more than 30 years in Jeff's body. That was double the life expectancy. It might have lasted another 30 years if Jeff's bones had been just as durable.

Jeff was discharged a few days later and sent to the rehab facility. He was there for two weeks before returning home to continue rehab with a home health care provider. The physical therapist came twice a week to assist and monitor his progress.

Meanwhile, I was tending to his postoperative drain and the 20 inch long incision. A nurse was also coming once a week to monitor his surgical site and assess his overall health. It was a huge relief when it was time to pull the drain from his wound. It had been a nuisance for him and a nightmare for me since I was responsible for its maintenance.

His right leg seemed to be healing well and his therapy was progressing. Jeff was very optimistic during this time. We had no reason to believe that the next surgery wouldn't prove just as beneficial. We settled in to enjoy the holidays with our family.

That's not to say that there weren't issues for us. He was still limited to a hospital bed or his wheel chair at all times. This made his daily activities, including hygiene, more difficult for both of us but we found a routine we could live with. It was not easy and we both longed for the day when, after the next surgery and rehab, he could be back on his feet again.

As much as he wanted to be done with the surgeries, he didn't want to go back to the hospital during the winter. He would have to be transported by gurney in an ambulance and didn't want to risk being exposed to the cold, wet weather prior to major surgery. We scheduled it for the spring.

Another activity that kept us both busy during the fall and winter of 2011 was watching our beloved Alabama football team. The players had suffered losses during the April tornado just like everyone else in Tuscaloosa. They had volunteered for searches and cleanup in the community. Watching them overcome adversity to win the BCS National Championship was a great distraction from our troubles and a beacon of hope for us and everyone in Tuscaloosa. We could rebuild the city and, Lord willing, the surgeon could rebuild Jeff's legs.

CHAPTER 20

13 Units

The left hip revision and rod insertion was scheduled for late April of 2012. Once again, the surgeon told us that it had been successful and saved the old prosthesis for us. We now had a matching pair of titanium hip implants. Jeff suggested that we make book ends out of them. We didn't but we did keep them on display in his room with some of his other treasures.

After a few days he was released and sent to the same rehab facility he had gone to before. There was no warning that he was about to have unexpected complications.

The rehab facility had an excellent reputation but they typically worked with sports injuries or similar issues in otherwise healthy people. They were not accustomed to patients with all of Jeff's physical limitations. This had not been a big problem during his first stay but it became evident during this visit.

On his second night there his drain became clogged, causing him a great deal of pain. He tried to explain to the nurses but they didn't take it very seriously. They didn't realize that when he admitted to being in pain, it meant he was in serious pain. After much persistence on his part, they finally sent him to a nearby emergency room. I made a midnight trip to Birmingham to meet him there and we agreed that he should not return to the rehab facility. After they treated the immediate problem in the ER he came home by ambulance to continue his therapy with the home health care therapist. However, our troubles were not over.

The drain in his leg was a continual source of concern for us. The drainage should have gradually slowed until the drain was no longer needed. The color of the fluid should also have paled to a light pink as the bleeding decreased. Neither of these things seemed to be happening.

Instead, after some weeks, the drain itself began to work its way out of the incision and he began to bleed around the site. I knew something was wrong but he stubbornly refused to go to the hospital. When the blood began pooling in the bed, I called our friend who was a nurse. She came over and, between us, we convinced him something had to be done.

He wanted to be taken back to his surgeon at UAB but his blood pressure was so low by this point that the ambulance attendants were required to take him to the nearest hospital to be stabilized first. They immediately began giving him blood transfusions to replace what he had been losing since the surgery.

We had no idea how critical he had become. He received 11 units of blood while at the local hospital before he could be sent to UAB to his surgeon. He received two more during the emergency surgery to repair his leg. A damaged blood vessel had been bleeding and caused a two liter hematoma or blood clot inside the tissue. The sheer size of it inside his leg had pushed the drain out. In total, he received 13 units of blood over four days. The human body only holds about 10 units.

After this near miss, he returned home to continue healing and rehabbing. He never lost sight of the goal of walking again and worked hard. He gradually became able to walk short distances in the house with a platform walker. This was a walker with attachments that allowed him to use his arms for strength and balance. This was much safer than using his crutches because it was a more stable apparatus but it still presented risks as it could tip over if he became unbalanced.

That is exactly what happened in the fall of that year. He became overbalanced to one side, hit the wall and slid to the floor. We got him into bed with the patient lift. He was shaken by the accident but we couldn't find any serious injury. The resulting nerve damage would become apparent over the next few months.

CHAPTER 21

75/25 Odds

Jeff began experiencing tingling and numbness in his arms and legs. It gradually worsened and by Christmas he could barely hold a pencil. We adapted his razor and other utensils with foam padding around the handles in an effort to give him a better grip.

By early February of 2013 he could no longer hold a spoon to feed himself. This was the last straw for him. He felt like his body was dying one piece at a time. We went back to the spine surgeon who had repaired his neck 17 years earlier.

This time the problem was more serious than a pinched nerve. Vertebrae in his neck had shifted and calcified so much that the blood flow to his spinal cord was being blocked. We saw x-rays of his entire spine at this time and it looked like a spiral staircase because the vertebrae were all twisting to one side. He had been experiencing some lower back pain but the immediate problem was in the neck area. The blockage had to be repaired or he would become paralyzed or worse.

The doctor warned us that this procedure was risky. There was a 25 percent chance that he wouldn't survive the surgery. Jeff was stunned. In all of his surgeries throughout his lifetime, he had never been given survival odds. In spite of this, he agreed to the surgery and it was scheduled for Friday, February 15th.

That morning I waited anxiously in Jeff's hospital room for word from the doctor about the outcome. The phone call came sooner than expected and I feared that something had gone wrong. As it turned out, they had been unable to perform the surgery. The anesthesiologist had been unable to intubate him and didn't want to risk losing him before they could get him connected to the respirator. He determined that they had to have a new plan before they tried again. Once more, they were fighting against the RA.

When Jeff got back to the room he was still groggy from the general anesthesia. I had to explain to him that they had not been able to do the surgery as planned. I wasn't sure if he would agree to a second attempt but he did. They did the procedure the next day on Saturday after the anesthesiologist came up with a custom designed protocol for Jeff. The surgery itself was a success. From that point forward, any time Jeff had surgery (and there were many more) we referred the anesthesiologist on his case to the notes in his chart about the special procedures.

CHAPTER 22

"Incompatible with Life"

After this major interruption to his therapy, he returned home in a neck brace and picked up where he left off. Of course, he was cautious with his neck but he was still determined to walk on his crutches again.

He continued the physical therapy on his platform walker. One day he reported to me that he had taken a few steps on his crutches during his session with the physical therapist while I was at work. For the first time in over two years, he felt "normal" again for a few minutes. We were thrilled with the progress. One day while Rachel was with us, he surprised us by standing up and taking a few steps with only his crutches for support. Rachel and I both cried for joy. It felt so strange to see my husband standing after so long of seeing him in a hospital bed or wheel chair. He seemed taller than I remembered. We all hoped that maybe, just maybe, recovery was possible.

He had worked so hard and come so close but it was not to be. After yet another fall from his platform walker, the tingling and numbness returned and worsened. The numerous falls and arthritic deformation had caused so much nerve damage that there was no repairing it. To add insult to injury, it had also caused incontinence. This determined man could no longer control his own bladder, even with a disposable urinal bottle constantly at his side.

He gave up hope of becoming ambulatory and tried to be content with moving around the house in his wheelchair. Even this became more difficult as the numbness increased and the pain from his damaged spine began worsening. He began spending more and more time in his bed.

We tried to deal with the issue of his incontinence with over-the-counter devices. He had no wish to see a doctor about the problem and we managed his hygiene over the next few months, not realizing that there was a deeper concern.

In early March of 2014, he began feeling unwell. In fact, one Sunday afternoon he called me into his room and asked me to just sit with him. This was very unusual and I tried to find out if something was wrong. As we sat quietly, he gradually began to give me clues about the pain and pressure he felt in his chest. I questioned him further, asking if I needed to call an ambulance. He insisted he didn't want to go to the hospital but he asked me to call Rachel and request that she come. By this time, I knew it was more serious than he was admitting but I called her and she got there as quickly as she could. I hoped she could get through to him where I failed.

With her arrival, he admitted that he thought it was his heart and that he was dying. He was indecisive about whether to seek medical help because he was so tired of fighting. He actually asked Rachel if he should keep fighting. I knew he was in turmoil or he would never have asked her such a question. She bravely answered that it was his decision.

He had never been in control of his health but he had always had the final word as to his healthcare. I would not take that away from him at this point and neither would she. Some people may question our decision but I knew how important that last shred of control was to him so I waited.

His speech gradually became slower and less precise. Throughout the afternoon we both sat with him. I informed him that it was his decision for now but the minute he could not speak to me coherently I was calling an ambulance. He finally gave in to the inevitable and agreed to go to the hospital. While we waited for the ambulance, I packed a few things and Rachel shaved his face for him. Even in distress, he wanted to keep some dignity.

We arrived at the hospital not a moment too soon. By the time we reached the emergency room he was in bad shape. I was allowed into the room with him to answer questions and comfort him. The doctor was frank with us and explained that some of his electrolytes were dangerously out of balance. In fact, his potassium was so high that it was "incompatible with life." Those were the doctor's exact words. He had indeed been on the verge of dying that afternoon from a potassium induced heart attack. Only our God in heaven knows how he had survived that long.

They quickly treated him to purge the potassium from his body and admitted him to the hospital. Thus began a three week hospitalization that would, once again, change his life.

After multiple tests and consultation with at least three specialists, it was determined that his kidneys were barely functioning and that had created the toxic levels of electrolytes. Several things could have led to this and it was most likely a combination of factors.

First, since he had become incontinent he had developed a severe kidney infection. His bladder was not fully emptying, which created a breeding ground for bacteria. This was alleviated by placing ureteral stents between his kidneys and bladder and by surgically implanting a supra-pubic catheter directly into his bladder through his abdomen. In essence, his urinary tract was replaced. This allowed the kidneys to heal and regain enough function that he did not have to go on dialysis at that time.

Other factors which posed a risk to his kidneys included the nerve damage in his spine, the fact that RA could have caused his own immune system to attack his organs and finally, the nonsteroidal anti-inflammatory drugs he had taken most of his life could have damaged his kidneys. Under attack from all sides, his kidneys didn't stand a chance.

From that point forward he would have to forgo the anti-inflammatory medicine which had slowed down the RA effects. This terrible disease could now cause pain and damage at will with nothing to stop it. Also, the catheter would have to be replaced monthly and the stents would be surgically replaced every six months.

He had survived once more but his routine was forever altered. He was so weak after his ordeal and three weeks in the hospital that he could barely sit up. He determined at that point that it wasn't worth the risk of trying to sit in his wheel chair. There would always be more falls and injuries. He would just remain bedfast as long as he lived. He didn't see this as giving up. To him, it was a rational, sensible decision and, since it was his choice, he accepted it more easily.

I believe he was also considering my welfare. He knew that it wasn't easy for me to hoist him in and out of bed and position him correctly in the chair. He also knew that he might need my care for a long time to come and anything that eased the physical strain on me now would prolong my ability to do that in the future.

His world had shrunk to our house at the time of his fall in 2011. Other than necessary trips by ambulance to the doctor or hospital, he had not left it. Now his world became his view from his hospital bed in his bedroom. He dreaded the surgeries every six months but he loved that he could see some new scenery during transport. He especially loved seeing the blue sky from his gurney as they wheeled him in and out of the ambulance. It was not visible from his bed.

His hospital bed had its own story to tell. The first one that we got in 2011 through insurance was the cheapest, simplest version you could get. It had no hand control for him and I actually had to turn a crank to raise or lower it. We lived with it for a while hoping this was a temporary situation but after several months he thought we needed something better.

He found out that his physical therapist had a used one he was willing to sell. It was a slightly better version with electronic controls. It was better in some ways but we had difficulty with the side rails, to the point of having to replace one of them. At that time we were using them constantly as he was moving in and out of bed frequently to his wheel chair or bedside toilet. We despaired of ever finding a good bed that we could afford.

That is when an old friend in Virginia learned of his need. Brenda had done well in her own business and loved him enough to simply send him a check for what he needed. He was forever grateful for her generosity. He found a refurbished bed that had originally been used in a hospital and had all the bells and whistles. He was excited.

Unfortunately, finding it was the easy part. He had paid for delivery to his bedroom but the driver was not able to get it into the house by himself. It was too big and bulky. Instead, it sat in our garage beside my car for three weeks until they could schedule a team of men to come and complete the delivery. I told him I needed a bumper sticker that said "my other car is a hospital bed."

They eventually did get it into his room. He enjoyed the hand controls that allowed him to position his bed for his comfort. It lasted several years before the motors died and we had to replace it with a simpler but newer model.

In 2015 another dear friend of ours passed away. Bernie had served as an elder with Jeff and they were very close. One day Bernie called as he was preparing to take a trip. They chatted a while and each told the other they loved him before hanging up. While on his trip, Bernie died suddenly when his heart stopped. By all accounts, he was talking one minute and gone the next. Like Jeff, Bernie was ready to go whenever the Lord called him home and Jeff was happy for him. He was actually a little envious that Bernie went so suddenly without any suffering. Jeff was not afraid of death but he did dread the suffering he would endure first.

Jeff was asked to say a few words for Bernie's memorial service. This was accomplished by way of a video recording. The recording shows Jeff sitting in his hospital bed at home, dressed in a hospital gown which he always wore. His thoughts are clear and his voice is strong as he tells of his relationship with Bernie. It was hard on him, both physically and emotionally, but he did it out of respect for his friend and fellow elder. He was still eager to serve others.

CHAPTER 23

Contentment

Jeff had long ago taken comfort in the Apostle Paul's words in Philippians chapter four where Paul says that he had learned to be content in all circumstances. If contentment was a learned behavior, then Jeff knew he could accomplish it. He lived by that all of his adult life, never more so than now.

He spent a lot of time on his laptop searching for bargains on the medical supplies we used and shopping for coins to add to his collection. He also became interested in arrowheads and began collecting them. I imagine this was a spinoff of his childhood rock collecting.

Another escape for him came from using computer apps to explore places he would never be able to visit. He could travel the world with just the touch of a button. At one point, he became fascinated with military bases across the country. He spent so much time looking at satellite photos that we joked about federal agents showing up on our doorstep demanding to know what he was doing.

This was not an easy life but we managed. He had two hospital style tables which we kept rolled over his bed, one from each side. With his limited arm movements it was difficult to keep everything within reach. He had an extended grabber tool, or "reacher," that he used constantly. He became as adept at using this as he had been with his crutches.

I was still working to supplement his disability income so I had to ensure he had everything he needed before I left the house. I would load his tables with his phone, laptop, water and snacks along with anything special he requested that day. It was a precarious way to leave him but he had his phone if he needed me and we could not afford any other solution.

During this time he had limited visitors by his own request. He usually did not feel up to entertaining friends. It was also painful for him emotionally to see the friends we had associated with in the past because it reminded him of all he had lost. They never realized it but any time he saw them, he cried after they left. He had been so brave for so long but now his memories and emotions could no longer be held at bay by hard work. One morning I found him crying when I went in to wake him. He had been thinking about the friends he lost as a child. I knew that hurt little boy was still living inside him.

One of his frequent visitors was my brother, Kenneth. He lived an hour away but enjoyed coming to talk with Jeff whenever he could. One morning in the wee hours, I received a call that Kenneth had died suddenly. I immediately went to Jeff. He had heard my sobs and knew it was bad. I sat on a stool beside his bed and laid my head against him while he comforted me. He stroked my head with hands which were permanently numb. He was still my rock when I needed him.

He always hated for anyone but me to take care of his personal hygiene but he suggested that Rachel stay with him for the day so that I could go to the funeral. He would risk the humiliation of having his daughter clean him, if necessary, while I was away. I needed to be with my family and I appreciated his sacrifice that allowed me to do that.

The few privileged visitors he agreed to see were blessed. He always appeared cheerful and many of them commented that they had come to encourage him but they always left feeling like he had encouraged them.

In spite of this ability to still encourage others, Jeff felt like his usefulness was over. It took another strange coincidence to remind him of his value.

Jeff's sisters, Sharon and Delores, had come down for a visit. They were discussing spiritual matters, as they often did when they were together, and Delores began telling Jeff of some of the work they were doing in her congregation. She had found some pamphlets in their library and they had begun using them in personal evangelism. As she described them, Jeff and I looked at each other. We both realized that these were the lessons he had created so many years ago. He had apparently given her a set and they had been rediscovered. It meant so much to him that his work could continue even after he was unable to leave his bed.

There were other happy events to break up the monotony. Rachel, Andrew and my sister, Oleta, usually spent holidays with us. We adapted by moving the celebration to his bedroom. We usually dined from trays but one Thanksgiving became memorable. He had recently bought a new hospital bed but the old one was still in his room. I pulled off the mattress, threw a tablecloth over the pan of the bed and we dined in style.

The most important event came in November of 2016. That's when our daughter gave birth to our grandson, Benjamin. We were unable to be with her in the hospital but they set up a video call with us as soon as he was born. They traveled down to see us the next week, in spite of the fact that it was not easy for Rachel to travel. I have a treasured photo of Jeff holding his look-alike grandson. That was the happiest I had seen him in years.

Still, the reality was that he was confined to his bed except for ambulance trips to the doctor or hospital. A nurse came once a month to change his catheter and draw blood. The blood draws were becoming more and more difficult and he was dreading them as much as the catheter changes. There were also the surgeries for stent replacements that had to be endured every six months. These were done as outpatient procedures but it made for a long, hard day and he always bled for a few days afterward.

He was also getting weaker all the time. He began having difficulty sitting up in bed. He fell to his right unless I kept pillows propped underneath and against his side. I later learned, by peeking at the doctor's notes, that this condition was call hemiplegia. If he wanted to reposition, I had to move his legs for him. He could not turn over by himself. The worsening nerve damage and constant inactivity was making it difficult for both of us. I gradually cut back on my work hours until I was only working 20 hours a week. Even then, I was not always there when he needed me.

The highlight of his week was when Rachel came to visit with Benjamin. At first, Jeff could not interact with him very much. Holding a newborn is a lot easier than holding a wiggly six month-old. As Benjamin grew older he was able to sit on the bed with Jeff. They played with his cars on Jeff's hospital table. Sometimes they watched

TV from Jeff's bed. Benjamin gradually began to understand that Grandpa's legs didn't work but that was alright because Grandpa was always smiling and laughing.

There were numerous other trips to the ER for various issues. None of them were life-threatening but all of them were troublesome. It was becoming painful for him to be handled and transported. We both tried to be content with our circumstances because we knew the next bad thing would happen and it would only get worse. We didn't know what or when but some other part of his body was going to wear out.

It wasn't long before we faced the next bad thing.

CHAPTER 24

To Dialyze or Not to Dialyze

In early February of 2018, Jeff began experiencing shortness of breath. It became so difficult to breathe that he could only sleep in a seated position. He finally agreed to go to the ER once more.

His kidneys had failed again. This time the fluid had built up around his heart and lungs making it difficult to breathe. He was admitted for treatment.

They gave him a dialysis treatment that first night. They drew off so much fluid that every muscle in his body began to cramp. For a few hours after the treatment he was in excruciating pain. The nurses assured him it was quite common to cramp after the first treatment but the next ones wouldn't cause that and they were correct. After a few treatments he was breathing easier and feeling better.

The question now became whether or not this was a permanent solution. The nephrologist wanted to see if his kidney function would rebound after receiving a little help. For 17 days they closely monitored his bloodwork and chest x-rays. He was also taking less frequent dialysis treatments to continue to alleviate the original symptoms. His kidney function remained border line.

The doctor finally decided that he should begin dialysis on a regular basis. Jeff could not face the prospect of being transported three times a week to the dialysis center. For him, the transport was worse than the treatment. If not for the option of home dialysis, I believe he would have refused any more treatment then and there. We had a lot to learn about it but peritoneal dialysis at home was the only choice that made sense for us.

Before he left the hospital, a surgeon implanted a peritoneal catheter into his abdomen. This catheter would be used to pump fluid in and out of the peritoneal cavity which would act as a filter in place of his kidneys. He would still take hemodialysis at the center for about three weeks until the catheter track had healed and was ready to use.

During the same surgery, they implanted a mediport into his chest for easier access to blood draws and IV's. Blood tests were going to be vital for monitoring his kidney function. He had become such a hard stick that it was simply impossible at times to draw blood.

He came home with a suprapubic catheter in his lower abdomen, a peritoneal catheter in his middle abdomen, a mediport in his left upper chest and a hemodialysis port in his right upper chest. Bathing him became an adventure.

While the peritoneal catheter was healing we had to be trained on the proper procedures for using the machine that would now be keeping him alive. I would be the one connecting him to the machine each night and disconnecting him and emptying bags in the morning. I would also maintain the catheter. There was a lot of cleaning and disinfecting involved since this represented a direct path to the inside of his body. I was overwhelmed at the responsibility of keeping him alive.

When I realized all that was involved I approached Jeff about the idea of my early retirement. It was becoming too complicated and too risky to leave him by himself for any length of time. We agreed that I would quit and we would somehow, with God's help, live on what we had.

Protocol required that Jeff go to the nephrologist's office once a month for monitoring. Because of the difficulty for us, the dialysis nurse graciously agreed to come to the house every month. Jeff would still have to be transported to see the doctor every three months but that was much more manageable. The regular home health care nurse was still coming once a month to change out the suprapubic catheter and she would do the necessary blood draws at that time.

The first few weeks of doing dialysis at home seemed a little overwhelming. The machine proved to be temperamental and alarms were going off each night. I would haul out the 150 page manual, find the problem and tinker with the tubing or bags of solution until the alarm was cleared. As we learned what to watch for, it became easier. Coordinating schedules, communicating with various agencies, ordering and picking up supplies became my full time job when added to Jeff's daily care but we were managing. We also enjoyed spending more time together now that I wasn't working outside the house.

During all that Jeff had suffered over the past several years, there wasn't a single hospital stay or ambulance transport where he didn't find some way to tell strangers about how blessed he was. He could be lying in bed with two broken legs and tell the doctor how good God is. He could be recovering from near fatal renal failure and mention to the dietician how much God had blessed him. Every housekeeper, maintenance worker, nurse or social worker that entered his room would hear about his blessings. No one was spared from hearing his testimony about our Lord.

That is not to say that he didn't have bad days. There were plenty of those but they usually occurred at home. There were a few occasions when he admitted to feeling like Job of Old Testament suffering fame. I would remind him that at least he had a better wife than Job's. He would smile and the moment would pass. We did our best to keep each other encouraged.

About this time, we had a conversation regarding his wedding ring. He had not been able to wear it for years due to the swelling in his hands. It sat safely in my jewelry box. I suddenly had an idea that was so simple that I don't know why I had never thought of it before. I suggested that I get his ring cut down so that I could wear it with mine. After all, his ring and my rings were a matched set, just like us. He loved the idea and I still wear them together to this day.

The dialysis worked well and gave us several more months together. He had more time to watch our grandson grow and develop and more time to have heart to heart talks with Rachel, his pride and joy. However, we both knew that life is fleeting and our time together on this earth was drawing to a close.

CHAPTER 25

The Long, Hard Summer

Jeff was scheduled for another stent replacement surgery in the middle of May, 2019. These were not pleasant but they had become routine and we knew what to expect. The ambulance transported him early that morning, as usual. I went with him to the holding area, as usual. After some time, they took him into surgery and I went to the waiting room, as usual.

I was expecting the usual phone call from the urologist but when it came it was not the usual message. He had managed to remove the old stents but could only get the new one into one side. Jeff's body had become so contorted and stiff with arthritis that it had become impossible to maneuver into the correct position.

I wasn't sure what this meant for Jeff's future and we talked further. When the urologist found out that Jeff was on dialysis he wanted to know why we were trying to save his kidneys with the stents. I was speechless because I hadn't realized that was what we were doing. I was irritated at the lack of communication between Jeff's doctors but what was done was done and we had to move forward with the new circumstances.

Apparently, the kidney without a stent would eventually die completely and the dialysis would pick up the extra load but what were we supposed to do about the other one when it was time to replace it in six months? I had no answers to give Jeff when he recovered from the anesthesia but it soon became obvious that we had a more immediate and urgent problem.

He was sent home by ambulance early in the afternoon. We began to notice that the output in the catheter bag was darker than normal. It was usually bright red for a day or so after the procedure then faded to pink before looking normal. This time it was dark red with noticeable clots. The tubing became clogged with the clots. We could not remove them regardless of how much we flushed it with sterile water. He was experiencing severe pain in his bladder from the buildup so we called an ambulance and went back to the hospital. The suprapubic catheter became completely dislodged during the transport due to the pressure.

The extreme difficulty of the procedure that day had created more trauma than normal. He was admitted and the doctors worked for five days trying to clear the excess blood and clots out of his system. One urologist suggested they rig up an irrigation system whereby fluid was forced into his bladder by one tube to be flushed out through his catheter. It was a messy and painful process and Jeff was more distressed than I had ever seen him. This was worse than all of his close calls with death.

He finally made it home again with a working catheter but his troubles were not over. A tooth had been broken during the anesthesia process and the rough edge was causing an ulcer on his tongue. He had not seen a dentist in years due to the difficulty of transport. Besides, the stiffness of his jaws prevented them from accessing much of his mouth.

A young dentist friend of ours agreed to drop by the house and have a look. There was little he could do other than reassure Jeff there was nothing else wrong in his mouth but that alleviated some of his worry. We tried to keep numbing medicine on his tongue and padding in his mouth until it healed.

This was just the latest in a series of ever mounting problems and Jeff became very pensive and withdrawn for several weeks. We continued with our daily routines but I could tell he had something weighing on his mind. I also knew he would tell me when he was ready and not before.

When he informed me that he had decided to stop the dialysis I was stunned but not surprised. It was just the type of brave decision he would make. I could tell he was at peace. After I dried a few tears, I asked if he was doing this for me, knowing that the caregiving was becoming physically harder on my body. I could not have born that. He admitted that was a small part of it but that was not his main concern.

He knew he would have died from natural causes if not for the dialysis and the dialysis was keeping him alive just to suffer. He knew the RA was making it impossible to perform necessary procedures. He knew there was evidence that other internal organs were being affected by the RA and it was just a matter of time before they began failing. Mostly, he knew he was tired of fighting a losing battle. He wanted to go home.

For Christians, this world is just a temporary stop on the way to our eternal home. No one believed that more than Jeff. For many years he kept a button over his car visor that read, "just visiting this planet." It had been manufactured and sold as a joke but he knew it to be true in a spiritual sense.

After the shock wore off I told him that I supported his decision and would do whatever he needed me to do. He wanted to take a few months to put his affairs in order before ending the treatment and would need my help. As usual, he had made a comprehensive list of things he needed to accomplish.

When Rachel visited again he told her of his plans. She was heartbroken but she also understood and agreed to support his decision. After that we began to tell our family and friends, who were also supportive. His doctors were taken aback with this turn of events but after speaking with him at length, they realized he had done his research and was at peace. They agreed to refer him to hospice care when the time came.

He set October 1, 2019 as his target date and got busy on his list.

Over the next few months, he made sure his will was current and discussed other legal documents with me. He updated his computer files so that I would have access to any information I needed. We also discussed his final arrangements.

He had planned many years earlier to donate his body to UAB for research. As we discussed the logistics of this it became apparent that it was going to be difficult for me to carry out his wishes. Instead, he decided to be cremated and left the details of the memorial service up to me. Personally, I was glad he changed his mind. His poor body had been sliced and diced, prodded, poked and photographed enough during his lifetime. I couldn't bear the thought of it enduring more indignities after his death.

Next on his list was the writing of thank you notes to anyone whom he felt had given us support over the last difficult years. There were twenty or more and it took us days. He dictated and I printed the letters for him to add his signature. He left instructions that they were not to be mailed until after his death. I agreed to his wishes but told him that I was glad I was not the one receiving a letter from a dead man.

One of his most important tasks was to write a letter for our grandson, to be opened when he turned 10 years old. It now resides in Rachel's safe. I suspect it is full of love, wit and wisdom.

Jeff was now experiencing even more constant pain and made it clear that he wanted no visitors aside from family and our minister. His sisters, Sharon and Delores, planned a trip from Virginia for the last of September. They wanted to see him one last time. They came and "sat at his feet" once more while discussing the Bible as they usually did.

While he was working on his final to do list, word was getting around about his decision. He began receiving cards and letters from many people we had known throughout the years. Without exception, they all spoke of the impact he had on them. This was so important for him.

Rachel and I had always tried to tell him that he was a special person and that he had made amazing accomplishments but he never truly believed it. His feeling of inadequacy persisted and even worsened after he became bedfast. Now he could see what he meant to so many other people and, for a little while, he saw himself as we saw him. I was thankful that he got to experience that.

These letters came from nieces and nephews who spoke of how he always listened to them, was always smiling, never complained and how he was their hero. They came from Rachel's friends who grew up watching his great example and yet felt included in his family. One such friend commented that he was inspired to "pursue higher things." They came from old friends who spoke of his great faith and wisdom and of the many Bible classes he taught. They came from newer friends who felt encouraged by his bravery and perseverance. They even came from people who had never met him but were inspired by his example. These letters were truly a blessing for Jeff in his final days and I will always be grateful for the many who took the time to write to him.

The many words of affirmation were wonderful but Jeff soon focused on a more serious job. He began mentally preparing for the great event of meeting his Creator.

CHAPTER 26

Victory!

Jeff had planned to have his last dialysis treatment on September 30th. A few days before that date we began having difficulty with the process. It didn't seem to be pulling off enough fluid over the course of the night. It left him feeling full and very uncomfortable. Either there was a problem with the equipment or his catheter or we needed a new prescription of the solution. It seemed as if Providence had stepped in once again to confirm his brave decision and take that burden from him. We agreed to stop the treatments on September 25th.

He could only be enrolled with hospice after the final treatment so we called them. We were very happy with their representatives and their approach. We felt that his final days would be as comfortable as possible.

Based on his research, he hoped that he wouldn't linger more than a few weeks after the last treatment. That was merely a guess because we had no way of knowing how much function he had left in his own kidneys.

After his sisters left we began to wait, watching for signs of renal failure. We stuck to our routine, minus the dialysis, but we were both on edge. This may have been the worst part of the whole ordeal. It must have been terrible for Jeff, waking each morning hoping to see evidence of his impending death. Even so, his sense of humor still made an appearance from time to time.

The hospice nurses came twice a week at this point but were available by phone whenever we needed them. They assured us they would come every day when his condition worsened. They also gave us the drugs that we would use to keep Jeff relaxed and comfortable at the end. I was not to administer them yet but they would be available when the time came.

God has always blessed me with good health and I seldom take medicine. In fact, Jeff used to tell me that I should go "lick an aspirin" if I had a headache because that was all I would need. I had prayed for strength each night and God had been with me for nearly nine years of taking care of Jeff without a sick day. Now suddenly I was hit with some kind of stomach bug at the worst possible time.

I called Rachel. She came down and we made arrangements to send Jeff to the hospice inpatient facility for what the insurance company called respite care. Rachel packed for him, helped him settle into his room and then came back to look after me.

Jeff and I both hated the fact that he had to leave because he wanted to die at home. Fortunately, after a few days I was strong enough to care for him again and we brought him home. There had been little change in his condition while he was gone.

After five weeks of no dialysis there was still very little evidence that his body was in trouble. He wasn't feeling very well and there was some bloating from fluid retention but nothing like what we had expected by this time. Apparently, his kidneys were stubborn, too.

On October 30th he began noticing some shortness of breath. We notified hospice and they began coming more frequently. They also gave me orders to begin using the drugs at four hour intervals. For the next week there was not much change. I was even able to leave him long enough to attend worship on Sunday, November 10th.

By Monday, the 11th, it was obvious he was declining. Rachel came down to stay and help for a few days. She was sleeping on the floor in his room on Monday night when he became very agitated and began hallucinating. It took more drugs and both of us to settle him for the remainder of the night. The dosage was not keeping pace with his decline and hospice gave me permission to give the drugs more frequently.

Early Tuesday morning, neither he nor Rachel could sleep much so she climbed up in his hospital bed with him and they laid there doing what they always did – talking. By the time I woke up, they had conspired together (something they also did frequently) for Rachel to pick up breakfast from a local café so we could eat together. Jeff always loved to eat, and eating breakfast together as a family was something he particularly enjoyed. He was more like himself but still had apparitions in his field of vision. He kept mentioning seeing something white float across the room. When we informed him that we didn't see anything, he joked that it must be the angels coming to take him home. He ate very little but seemed to enjoy our time together. This would be his last meal.

Tuesday afternoon the power went off in our neighborhood for a few hours. It was impossible to make him understand why we couldn't raise or lower his electric bed to make him more comfortable. He was sleeping most of the time now, courtesy of the drugs, which was just how he had planned it.

Rachel and I were taking turns sitting with him. When we had time we were busy preparing the syringes with the drugs provided by hospice. These were applied to the inside of his cheek since he could no longer swallow. Friends had begun bringing meals so we could focus on caring for him. They had wanted to do something to help for years but I had always told them we could manage. Now they held nothing back. We ate well.

On Thursday my sister, Oleta, came down to stay and help with the sitting duties and Andrew came to bring Rachel more clothes. She couldn't bring herself to leave at this point. Jeff roused up enough to earnestly ask Rachel if he was going to die that day. Looking at his face, she knew he wanted a truthful answer. She told him she wasn't sure, but that if he did, he was ready and he would be ok.

He uttered his final coherent words later that morning when he woke and saw Andrew standing by my chair. He looked at Andrew and said "Take care of her. She's a good woman." As expected, his final concerns were for me.

Friday and Saturday brought more labored breathing and more frequent doses of drugs to keep him comfortable. We could see the steady decline in his condition but he seemed to be unaware of his surroundings most of the time.

Sunday morning, November 17th, Jeff's three surviving siblings were gathered together in one place. They called and wanted to tell him goodbye. I held the phone to his ear while each of them spoke to him. He gave no sign of responding to their voices but we'll never know if he heard. Hospice nurses will tell you that hearing is one of the last things a dying patient loses. That's why it is important to keep talking to them.

Later that morning I was sitting with him while Rachel slept after taking her night shift. Around 11 o'clock I noticed a specific breathing pattern that, according to the hospice literature, meant that death was coming soon. I called for Rachel and Oleta to come in. We gathered around his bed and watched as his respirations became slower and shallower.

On that bright Sunday morning, while his brothers and sisters in Christ were worshiping our Lord, his beautiful spirit was finally set free to see Him face to face. His spirit was no longer imprisoned in a body filled with pain. He could now worship our Savior in a way that we can only imagine here on earth.

Rachel threw herself onto his lifeless chest and exclaimed, "You did it, Dad. You did it!"

What a perfect epitaph! He had indeed done it. He had done more with his broken body than most healthy people ever dream of doing. In spite of tragedy, loss, illness, pain and disability, he had lived well and died without fear, trusting his Lord till the end.

If he could have spoken then, I think he would have quoted the Apostle Paul's words to Timothy in II Timothy chapter four. "I have fought the good fight, I have finished the course, I have kept the faith; in the future there is laid up for me the crown of righteousness, which the Lord, the righteous Judge, will award to me on that day; and not only to me, but also to all who have loved His appearing."

CHAPTER 27

Lasting Legacy

When a pebble is dropped into calm water, it creates ever widening circles of ripples. The farther away the ripple, the less power and energy it has. It is still noticeable, nonetheless.

That was Jeff's life. Every life he touched was somehow made better. They were encouraged or inspired or just made into better people. I was no exception.

Jeff told me once that he could appreciate why God brought me into his life because he needed me. What he couldn't understand was why God brought him into mine. I told him that God knew I needed to learn to be a servant. That was true but not the whole truth. From Jeff I learned about courage, contentment, kindness and so much more. Mostly, I just became a better person by living with him.

I wanted more people to benefit from his example so, for his memorial, I asked the minister to just tell of Jeff's amazing life and how God's grace had always been there. Our friends and family had all heard parts of his story but they were reminded and amazed all over again. For those who had never met him but came out of respect for our family, they were astonished and inspired at hearing it for the first time. As of the time of this writing, two years later, people still come to me and speak of how encouraging his memorial service was to them.

For you readers who were never blessed to meet him, I have tried to create a glimpse of him so that you may find encouragement and inspiration as well. He never realized how important his example was but he would be happy to know that his story might still help a fellow human being, especially if it brought them closer to our Lord.

About a year after his death, I received some pictures that Sharon had taken on their final visit. She had captured a very somber expression on Jeff's face. At first glance, I was distressed because I thought he looked so sad. Then I studied it more closely. I realized Jeff's face was an outward expression of the yearning in his spirit. His spirit was looking for the door to eternity. It was a longing for home that I saw in his eyes. I smiled then because I knew he had found it.

The white box still sits on my closet shelf. Rachel and I have discussed possible resting sites but have decided to keep his remains close. His spirit belongs to God, his story belongs to the world but his physical remains and beloved memory belong to us. We're blessed to have them.

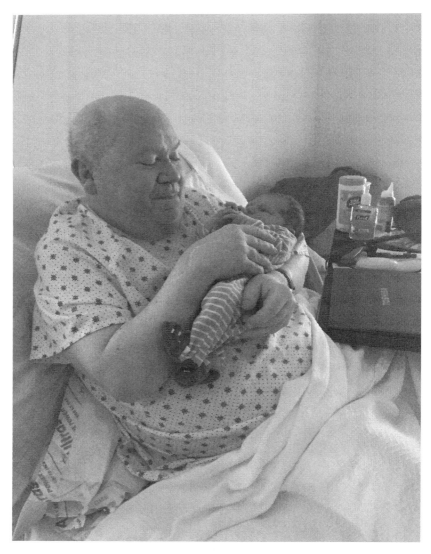

Proud Grandpa meeting Benjamin

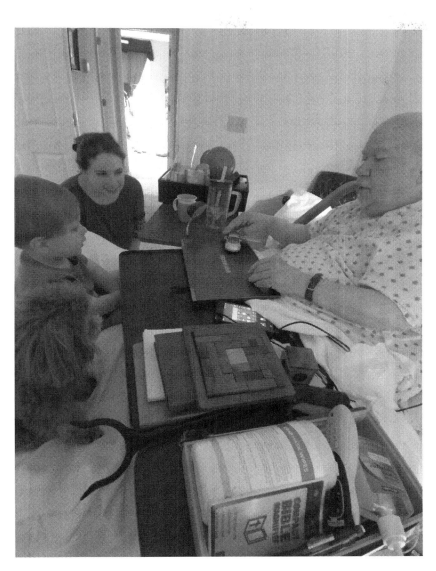

Playing with Benjamin in bed

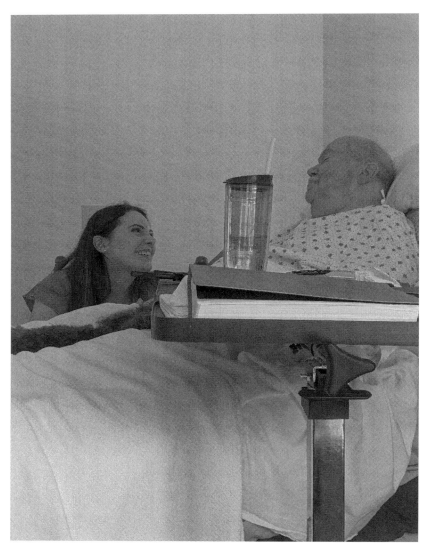

Jeff and Rachel share a special moment

Ronnie, Jeff, Sharon and Delores

Made in United States
Orlando, FL
21 December 2022

27425304R00086